CAMINO BOOKS
THE BEST OF THE BOOK & THE COOK

Phyllis Stein-Novack is a food and wine journalist, author and critic whose work has appeared in *USA Today,* the *Philadelphia Daily News*, and other publications. She currently writes the Tasting column for *Mid Atlantic Country* magazine.

She is a member of Les Dames d'Escoffier, The Women's Culinary Guild and lives in center city Philadelphia with her husband, Edward.

Bon Appetit

Phyllis Stein-Novack

The Best of the Book & the Cook:

Great Menus and Recipes by America's Most Talented Cookbook Authors

Text by Phyllis Stein-Novack

Foreword by Julie Dannenbaum
Concept by Lenora Berson

CAMINO BOOKS
Philadelphia

Manufactured in the United States of America

1 2 3 4 5 93 92 91 90

Library of Congress Cataloging-in-Publication Data

The best of the Book & the Cook: great menus and recipes by America's most talented cookbook authors / by Phyllis Stein Novack. p. cm.
1. Cookery. 2. Menus. 3. Restaurants, lunch rooms, etc. — Pennsylvania—Philadelphia. I Title. II. Title: Best of the book and Cook.

TX714.S75 1990 641.5—dc20 90-1384
ISBN 0-940159-07-4

For Information write:

Publisher
Camino Books, Inc.
P.O. Box 59026
Philadelphia, PA 19102

Permissions to reproduce the recipes can be found beginning on page 180

Cover & Text designed by: Amy Blake

Contents

ACKNOWLEDGEMENTS

This book was commissioned by the Office of the City Representative, City of Philadelphia.

Mayor W. Wilson Goode would like to acknowledge invaluable aid given to the development of this unique volume by: Phyllis Polk, Judy Faye, Bunny Baum, Herbert Popper, Jan Kaminsky, Jacques Petersen, Patricia McErlean, Miranda Beebe and Lily Hsu.

FOREWORD

I have always been a champion of Philadelphia restaurants.

Philadelphians do eat out and Philadelphians do support good restaurants. They supported my cooking school which I opened in 1964. For more than 20 years, I experienced first-hand how eager Philadelphians were to learn about food.

I have followed the food scene in this city from my early Horn & Hardart automat days of the 1940s right up to today. Besides the automat, I have fond memories of Kugler's downstairs on Chestnut Street near Caldwell's, which had individual rooms, each serving a different foreign cuisine. Shoyer's was a nifty family place with genteel old waiters. If I had a yen for mussels, I headed for South Philadelphia, and went to Chinatown to satisfy the desire for egg rolls. Helen Siegel Wilson did her share early on to expose Philadelphians to quiche, coq au vin and brioche—served at her restaurant on Walnut Street where Le Bec-Fin is now. If I were in the mood for music, I went to the Warwick Hotel and enjoyed shrimp lamaze during the tea-dance. In Society Hill, Jeannine and Janine, the very first French restaurant this city ever had, offered beef bourguignon and chocolate mousse.

But wonderful as the old days were, I think Philadelphia restaurants have never been better. Any kind of food I hanker for can be found in the City of Brotherly Love. I can dine in truly elegant surroundings or have a snack at a bistro or a bar. There are cafes, bistros, and New Orleans-style places. I can enjoy a meal in a garden or on the water. I have my choice of Italian trattorias, whether northern, southern, or in between. If I want Californian, Southwest, or Mexican, it is all here. French, Spanish, Thai, or East meets West—I know where to go.

Philadelphia is exciting and becoming more so. Our restaurants are enticing and add more to adventurous dining every year.

So I am not surprised that The Book and the Cook was created in Philadelphia. This annual fete brings cookbook authors from all over the world and pairs them with Philadelphia restaurants. It's a brilliant idea!

I hope it continues forever.

Julie Dannenbaum

INTRODUCTION

The Book and the Cook is a unique long weekend of fine dining in Philadelphia. Launched in 1985, it pairs world famous cookbook authors and wine authorities with Philadelphia chefs, restaurateurs, and caterers to create one-of-a-kind meals and wine-tasting events open to the general public.

Adding to the flavor of the weekend is the presence of the celebrity authors, who meet and talk with diners. The writers discuss their food and wine philosophies when their special menus are served.

Interestingly, The Book and the Cook started as a political campaign promise. In 1983, during his first campaign for Mayor, W. Wilson Goode made a public commitment to use the city government's ability to generate publicity to promote Philadelphia's growing restaurant industry.

Although in the 1970s Philadelphia had begun to develop a cadre of world-class restaurants, like other assets of this understated metropolis, it was a well-kept secret. But it was a secret the new Goode Administration wanted to tell because tourists are often lured to a city by its restaurant reputation.

Thus, in the spring of 1984, at the mayor's direction, a task force was formed composed of representatives of the city government, the Convention and Visitor's Bureau, the Philadelphia-Delaware Valley Restaurant Association, the major hoteliers, and their public relations agencies.

This group reviewed a variety of promotional events carried out by Philadelphia and other cities, particularly large-scale outdoor public restaurant festivals and collaborative restaurant gourmet banquets. The overwhelming response of those in the restaurant business was that, while the general public greatly enjoyed these events, they did not bring new customers into their restaurants nor generate favorable national publicity for them.

Next, the task force discussed the positive effect of national food writers' conventions on the public hospitality image of the cities in which they were held. Because these conventions move their site each year, it did not seem practical to look to them as a major ongoing source of promotion. But the discussion sparked an idea. Restaurateur Judy Wicks of the White Dog Cafe noted that "cookbook authors are new celebrities. In addition to writing books, they also write for newspapers and magazines and appear on television shows around the country." Therefore she suggested we "bring cookbook authors to Philadelphia, introduce them to Philadelphia's restaurants and they will spread the word about our restaurants' quality."

Just how to introduce the cookbook authors became the project of the Office of the City Representative, Philadelphia's official marketing and promotional agency.

The first step was to invite nationally known cookbook authors to the city on an honorarium basis for a weekend in 1985. March was chosen because it is one of the slowest months in the hotel calendar. The specifics of the program, however, were left vague because they were vague.

The first author to accept was Craig Claiborne. This gave credibility to the idea. By September 1984, a prestigious group of authors including Maida Heatter, Julie Dannenbaum, Martha Stewart, Helga Rubinstein, and Jonathan Waxman agreed to participate.

The question was what to do with the celebrities when they came to town. Keeping in mind that the restaurateurs wanted customers coming to their restaurants, not attending seminars and conferences, it was decided to pair each author with a compatible restaurant to collaborate with the chef on a one-of-a-kind meal to be served in the restaurant. The public would be invited to reserve seats at this meal which would be served on a fixed-price basis. The author would meet and talk with the dining patrons.

At first many restaurants were hesitant to join the program, but the strong support given by Kathleen Mulhern of The Garden, Steve Poses of Shooting Stars, Judy Wicks of White Dog Cafe, Judi DiVicaris of Cafe Nola, Georges Perrier of Le Bec-Fin, and David Mink of Sansom Street Oyster House (then head of the Philadelphia Delaware Valley Restaurant Association) insured strong restaurant participation.

The most ticklish part was, and is, matching authors and restaurants. Some matches are obvious and easy: Craig Claiborne asked to be placed at Le Bec-Fin and George Perrier welcomed Claiborne, a long-time personal friend and supporter, with open arms. Steve Poses bid on the knowledgeable and voluble Barbara Kafka, partly because she was his cousin. The Garden offered a perfect setting for elegant Anne Willan.

Other pairings were less obvious, but no less successful. For example, Howard Mitchum, who claims to know how to cook an alligator, played to a packed Sansom Street Oyster House, though his menu served up tamer fare.

Some pairings are suggested by restaurateurs, others are initiated by invited authors requesting particular restaurants. Most of the couplings, however, are made by the Office of the City Representative.

City officials try to find authors and restaurants with similar palates. Marcella Hazan, who helped design the original menu for DiLullo's restaurant in the Fox Chase section of Philadelphia, was an obvious choice for that location. Louise Szathmary, an author known for his Hungarian specialties, was a subtle but wonderful partner for Chef Fritz Blank's old Deux Cheminees. Both share a passion for good local provender. Paula Wolfert was a natural for Odeon, a Parisian bistro set in Center City Philadelphia; while Vertamae Grosvenor of Vibration Cooking fame made a homecoming appearance at Mama Rosa's. Long-term partners include Eileen Yin Fei-Lo and Susanna Foo, while Giuliano Bugialli pays repeated visits to Il Gallo Nero.

From its first appearance in 1985, The Book and the Cook has been a sellout event. Many diners come back year after year. Starting with twenty-seven authors and twenty-six restaurants, it has expanded to sixty-six authors and food experts, fifty-nine restaurants, and four catering firms.

Meals and wine-tastings are annually attended by more than 10,000 patrons. Not incidentally, The Book and the Cook also sells large numbers of its guest authors' cookbooks.

The progress of the event mandated the publishing of a cookbook to share these special meals with a far larger audience than can be accommodated over one long weekend in March. The result is this book. It represents the best of The Book and the Cook's five years. In some instances, we were unable to obtain an author's or publisher's permission to print recipes. In other cases, the similarity of menus dictated the choice of one menu over another. We eliminated some wonderful and unique meals because they were simply too long and too complicated. The large number of splendid menus from which to choose also allowed us to make personal selections. We have tried to present a diverse collection in all modes and styles, not only to offer the home cook a wonderfully varied selection, but also to demonstrate the great range and depth of our city's restaurant capabilities.

We have greatly enjoyed putting together this book of memorable meals, and we wish you equally happy hours in your kitchen reproducing them.

Lenora E. Berson
Director of Special Projects

WORDS FROM THE MAYOR

The Best of The Book and the Cook is a compilation of menus and recipes created by a unique collaboration between the world's most celebrated cookbook authors and Philadelphia's leading chefs and restaurateurs. These menus and recipes form the centerpiece of The Book and the Cook, Philadelphia's annual celebration of its fine restaurants.

Initiated in 1985, The Book and the Cook has brought more than 60 taste-setting food writers and celebrities to Philadelphia. The event takes place over a long weekend in March. It offers patrons of our restaurants not only an opportunity to eat an extraordinary meal, but also a chance to meet and discuss it with the culinary experts who have created it.

The success of The Book and the Cook testifies to the quality, number, and variety of local eating establishments. There is a fine restaurant in Philadelphia to match every palate and every pocketbook. Represented in this book are meals served in classic French restaurants, Italian restaurants, Cajun restaurants, neighborhood ethnic restaurants, and even in diners.

Scattered across the city, purveyors of fine public fare can be found in every section of Philadelphia, from the heart of the Italian Market to the hills of Manayunk, from the far reaches of the Northeast to the elegant Benjamin Franklin Parkway.

Philadelphia's tradition of good food goes back to the days when we were the crown city of the English colonies. We were then, as we are now, known not only for the quality of our public fare, but also for the elegance of our private tables.

This tradition actually played a part in history. During the summer of 1787, the leading delegates to the Constitutional Convention dined every night in the home of Benjamin Franklin. There, over spit-roasted meats, root vegetables, and port, they continued to discuss and refine the Articles of the Constitution.

It is our pleasure to share with the readers of this book the secrets and delights of Philadelphia's Book and the Cook. We hope that it will tempt you to eat in our wonderful restaurants and inspire you to cook great meals in your own kitchen.

W. Wilson Goode
Mayor of Philadelphia

The Best of the Book & the Cook:

Jean Anderson is the preeminent American authority on Portuguese cuisine. Her book *The Food of Portugal* is the major book on Portuguese cooking written in English. It won a Tastemaker Award and it takes its readers on a tour of this singular Iberian nation.

Jean Anderson is the author of more than a dozen other cookbooks. She writes regularly for food and travel magazines, and the photographs she takes often accompany her words.

Anderson and chef/proprietor James Sherman prepared this authentic Portuguese dinner at Jamey's on March 17, 1988. The recipes are from *The Food of Portugal.*

Jamey's is located in the Manayunk section of Philadelphia. It is housed in a reconverted store on Main Street, a popular business strip of low two-and-three story 19th century brick buildings. Its tin hammered ceiling and old-fashioned wood bar are illuminated by art deco-style lamps set off by post-modern pastel pinks and greens. The food is a mixture of New American, Italian and Portuguese favorites. Fresh fish and fowl are also featured. Understated but smart, Jamey's caters to the young professionals who are rapidly transforming this once ethnic neighborhood into a hot real estate market.

GREEN SOUP

(Caldo Verde)

PORK WITH CLAMS ALENTEJO-STYLE

(Porco a Alentejana)

STEAMED WHITE RICE

CARAMELIZED FLAN FROM PINHAO

(Pudim Flan de Pinhao)

Vinho Verde
Dao Grao Vasco
Serves 6

GREEN SOUP *(Caldo Verde)*

1 large yellow onion, peeled and minced fine
1 large garlic clove, peeled and minced
4 tablespoons olive oil
6 large Maine or Eastern potatoes, peeled and sliced thin
2 quarts cold water
6 ounces chourico, chorizo, pepperoni or other dry garlicky sausage, sliced thin
2 1/2 teaspoons salt (about)
1/4 teaspoon freshly ground pepper
1 pound collards, kale or turnip greens, washed, trimmed of coarse stems and veins, then sliced filament-thin. (The easiest way is to stack 6 to 8 leaves, roll crosswise into a firm, tight roll, then slice with a very sharp knife.)

1. Sauté the onion and garlic in 3 tablespoons of the oil in a large heavy saucepan 2 to 3 minutes over moderate heat until they begin to color and turn glassy; do not brown or they will turn bitter.
2. Add the potatoes and sauté, stirring constantly, 2 to 3 minutes, until they begin to color also. Add the water, cover and boil gently over moderate heat 20 to 25 minutes until the potatoes are mushy.
3. Meanwhile, fry the sausage in a medium-size heavy skillet over low heat 10 to 12 minutes until most of the fat has cooked out; drain well and reserve.
4. When the potatoes are soft, remove the pan from the stove and with a potato masher, mash the potatoes right in the pan in the soup mixture. Add the sausage, salt and pepper, return to moderate heat, cover and simmer 5 minutes. Add the collards and simmer uncovered 5 minutes until tender and the color of jade. Mix in the remaining tablespoon of olive oil and taste the soup for salt and pepper.
5. Ladle into large soup plates and serve as a main course accompanied by chunks of Broa (Portuguese bread).

PORK WITH CLAMS ALENTEJO-STYLE
(Porco a Alentejana)

2 1/2 pounds boneless pork loin, cut into 1-inch cubes
A paste made of 1 peeled and crushed garlic clove, 1 teaspoon kosher salt, 1 tablespoon paprika (preferably the Hungarian sweet rose paprika), and 1 tablespoon olive oil.
1 cup dry white wine
2 large bay leaves, crumbled
2 tablespoons olive oil
2 tablespoons lard (hog lard, not vegetable shortening)
1 large yellow onion, peeled and coarsely chopped
1 large garlic clove, peeled and minced
2 tablespoons tomato paste
18 small littleneck clams in the shell, scrubbed well and purged of grit. (To do this, cover the clams with cold water, add 1 tablespoon cornmeal, let stand at room temperature 20 to 30 minutes, then drain well.)
1/4 teaspoon salt (about)
1/4 teaspoon freshly ground black pepper (about)

1. Rub the pieces of pork well all over with the paste and place in a large, shallow nonmetallic bowl; add the wine and bay leaves, cover and marinate about 24 hours, turning the pork occasionally in the wine.

2. Next day, heat the olive oil and lard in a large heavy kettle over high heat until ripples appear on the kettle bottom - the fat should "almost" smoke. Lift the pork from the marinade (save the marinade to add to the kettle later) and brown in 3 batches, transferring pieces to a large heat-proof bowl as they brown.

3. When all the pork is brown, dump the onion and garlic into the kettle, lower the heat to moderate and stir-fry 3 to 4 minutes until limp and golden. Turn the heat to low, cover the kettle and and steam the onion and garlic 20 minutes.

4. Blend in the tomato paste and reserved wine marinade, return the pork to the kettle, adjust the heat so that the wine mixture barely bubbles, then cover and cook 1 1/2 hours until the pork is fork-tender. Now bring the kettle liquid to a gentle boil, lay the clams on top of the pork, distributing them as evenly as possible, re-cover and cook about 30 minutes - just until the clams open, spilling their juices. Season to taste with salt and pepper and ladle into large soup plates over steamed rice.

CARAMELIZED FLAN FROM PINHAO
(Pudim Flan de Pinhao)

Caramelized Sugar Syrup:
1/2 cup sugar
1/2 cup boiling water
Flan:
2 cups half-and-half cream
2 cups heavy cream
1 cup sugar
4 strips orange zest, each about 2 inches long and 1/2-inch wide
2 tablespoons caramelized sugar syrup
12 jumbo egg yolks
1/4 cup tawny port

For the caramelized sugar syrup:

1. Place the sugar in a medium-size heavy skillet (not iron), set over moderately low heat and allow to melt and caramelize to a rich golden brown (this will take about 40 minutes). Do not stir the sugar as it melts but do shake the skillet from time to time.
2. Add the boiling water, teaspoon by teaspoon at first, stirring briskly to dissolve the caramelized sugar. Simmer uncovered 8 to 10 minutes until the consistency of maple syrup.
3. Reserve 2 tablespoons of the caramelized sugar syrup for the flan; pour the balance into a chilled, well-buttered, shallow fluted 2-quart mold. Set the mold in the freezer while you prepare the flan.

For the flan:

1. Preheat the oven to moderately low (325 degrees). Combine the half-and-half, heavy cream and sugar in a large heavy saucepan; drop in the orange zest and bring to a simmer over moderately low heat, stirring now and then; blend in the 2 tablespoons of reserved caramelized syrup.
2. Beat the egg yolks until frothy; blend 1 cup of the hot cream mixture into the yolks, stir back into the pan and heat, stirring constantly, 1 minute. Remove from heat and mix in the port.
3. Strain all through a fine sieve, then pour into the prepared mold. Set the mold in a shallow baking pan and pour in enough hot water to come halfway up the mold. Bake uncovered 1 1/2 hours or until a toothpick inserted near the center of the flan comes

out clean. Remove from the oven and the water bath; cool 1 hour, then refrigerate 4 to 5 hours until firm.

4. To invert the flan, dip the mold quickly in hot water, then turn out on a dessert plate with a turned-up rim; the caramel syrup will come cascading down over the flan. Cut into slim wedges.

Craig Claiborne is the dean of American food writers. For the past 30 years his views and philosophy on American and international cuisine, along with profiles of celebrated chefs and restaurateurs, have been a mainstay of The New York Times.

A native of Sunflower, Mississippi, Claiborne is the author of nineteen cookbooks including *Craig Claiborne's Memorable Meals*, *The New York Times Cookbook*, and *Craig Claiborne's Southern Cooking*.

The following luncheon, served on March 26, 1987, consisted of several Claiborne favorites created by Georges Perrier, chef/proprietor of Le Bec Fin.

Le Bec Fin is a four star restaurant located in the city's business district. Its cozy bar and elegant dining room are beautifully set off by fine linen, Christofle silver and fresh flowers. Chef/proprietor Georges Perrier offers a fixed price dinner from which diners can choose appetizers, fish, main entrees of game, fish and fowl, salad, cheese and selections from the famous dessert cart.

Sommelier Gregory Moore aids in the selection of fine wines from around the world.

SALAD OF ASSORTED GREENS WITH MAYONNAISE

(Salad de la Maison)

DUCK MOLDS WITH ROUENAISE SAUCE

(Tians de Canard avec Sauce Rouenaise)

CASSIS SORBET

(Sorbet au Cassis)

Sonoma Cutrer Chardonnay Les Pierres, 1986

(or any good white burgundy)

Fixin Huguenot, 1985

(or any good red burgundy)

Chateau Lafaurey Peyraguey Lafaurie, 1981

(or any good sauterne)

Serves 6

DUCK MOLDS *(Tians de Canard)*

2 pounds spinach, cleaned
2 tablespoons butter
12 tomatoes, peeled, seeded and coarsely chopped
12 tablespoons oil
2 pounds shiitake mushrooms, sliced
8 (1-pound) duck breasts, skin and bones removed

1. Sauté spinach in butter, add salt and pepper to taste, drain and set aside.
2. Sauté tomatoes in 2 tablespoons very hot oil, season with salt and pepper, and set aside to cool.
3. Sauté mushrooms in 2 tablespoons very hot oil, add salt and pepper to taste and set aside.
4. Set 12 (4-inch) ring molds on a baking sheet. Layer spinach, tomatoes and mushrooms into the molds and set aside.
5. Season duck breasts with salt and pepper and sear in 8 tablespoons hot oil. Bake in a 400-degree oven for 10 minutes. Remove from oven and slice lengthwise in very thin strips.
6. Place vegetable molds into a 400-degree oven for 5 minutes until hot. Remove rings and place vegetables on plates. Cover with duck strips and top with Sauce Rouenaise.

SAUCE FOR DUCK MOLDS *(Sauce Rouenaise)*

2 carrots, chopped
1 stalk celery, chopped
1 onion, peeled and chopped
5 tablespoons oil
2 pounds roasted duck bones and carcass
3 liters red wine
1 1/2 gallons duck stock
5 chicken livers, chopped

1. Cook vegetables in large pot in oil until they start to brown. Add bones and wine. Turn the heat very low, let the wine come to a boil and ignite to burn off the alcohol. Reduce the liquid to 1 cup.
2. Add duck stock and cook slowly for 1 hour. Remove the bones and crush them with a wooden spatula, put them back in the pot and cook another hour.
3. Put the chicken livers and 2 tablespoons of the sauce into a food processor, process them and place them back into the sauce.
4. Cook 20 minutes more, pass through a china cap sieve and set aside. Warm on low heat when ready to use.

Makes about 1 gallon of sauce. Can be frozen for later use.

CASSIS SORBET *(Sorbet au Cassis)*

3 cups black currants
1 cup plus 2 tablespoons sugar
1 1/2 cups water, divided
2 tablespoons cassis liqueur
1 tablespoon fresh lemon juice
3 tablespoons whipping cream

1. Place the black currants in a medium-size saucepan. Sprinkle with sugar, add 1/2 cup of the water, and the cassis liqueur. Simmer about 15 to 20 minutes, or until the currants are tender and almost puréed.
2. Place the currant mixture with its syrup, the lemon juice, and cream in the bowl of a food processor fitted with the steel blade. Process until smooth. Taste for sweetness and adjust with more lemon juice or sugar, if necessary. Remove the mixture from the food processor and stir in the remaining 1 cup of water.
3. Freeze the mixture in an ice cream maker, following the manufacturer's directions.

Makes 1 quart

Jack Czarnecki is a chef, restaurateur and expert in mycology - that branch of botany which focuses on fungi, or in culinary terms - mushrooms.

The Czarnecki family has presided over Joe's in Reading, Pennsylvania for 72 years. Jack Czarnecki, who has been proprietor since 1978, enjoys walks in the woods with his wife and children, searching for 30 types of wild mushrooms which turn up on the menu at Joe's. He is the author of *Joe's Book of Mushroom Cookery*.

This menu was created jointly by Jack Czarnecki and Chef John Jividen of Ridgewell's Caterers and was served at the Academy of Natural Sciences on March 27, 1987. The recipes for the roast chicken breast and mushroom salad are from *Joe's Book of Mushroom Cookery*. The dessert is chef Jividen's creation.

Ridgewell's, the largest on-site catering firm in the United States, has catered inaugural balls, prepared special embassy dinners, and was recently appointed by Donald Trump to cater many of the parties on his yacht, the Trump Princess. They have catered parties for the Constitution Bicentennial as well as the private sector.

The company was founded in 1928 by Charles Ridgewell, a former butler at the British Embassy. Since then, the firm has expanded into the Philadelphia area with offices in King of Prussia and Society Hill.

MENU

**ROAST CHICKEN BREAST
WITH BLACK TRUMPET SAUCE**

**WILD AND WHITE RICE WITH APRICOTS,
CHANTERELLES AND SUMAC**

STEAMED FRESH GREEN PEAS

**SALAD OF MARINATED LACTARIUS
MUSHROOMS WITH ARUGULA**

GRAND MARNIER SOUFFLÉ

Cabernet Sauvignon

Serves 4

ROAST CHICKEN BREAST WITH BLACK TRUMPET SAUCE

For the Sauce:
1 ounce dried black trumpet mushrooms
2 cups water
1 tablespoon salt
1/2 tablespoon sugar
1 tablespoon scallions
1/2 tablespoon fresh, crushed ginger
1 tablespoon arrowroot, mixed with 1/4 cup water
For the Chicken:
4 chicken breasts
Salt and pepper to taste

1. Combine mushrooms with water, salt, and sugar in a saucepan, bring to a boil. Simmer for about 15 minutes, until liquid is down to 1 1/2 cups.
2. Shift mushrooms and liquid to a saucepan with a tight-fitting lid. Add scallions and ginger.
3. Thicken this mixture with arrowroot and water mixture until liquid is lightly thickened.
4. Simmer on low heat and keep warm while chicken is cooking.
5. Preheat the oven to 350 degrees. Wash and dry the chicken breasts, place in pan and add salt and pepper to taste. Roast about 25 minutes or until lightly brown.
6. Remove to warm plates and top with sauce.

WILD AND WHITE RICE WITH APRICOTS, CHANTERELLES AND SUMAC

1/2 cup raw wild rice
1/2 cup white long grain rice
Water to cover
3 cups water
1 teaspoon salt
1 tablespoon butter for preparing the rice
1/3 cup chopped onions
3 tablespoons butter, divided
1 1/2 cups fresh chanterelles, sliced, or 1/2 cup canned chanterelles, drained and sliced
2 tablespoons chopped dried apricots
1/2 tablespoon salt
Sumac for garnish

1. Wash the rice, cover with water and soak for 30 minutes. Drain off water and rinse in cold water.
2. Bring water, salt and butter to boil in a saucepan. Add rice. Cover and cook until rice grains are just tender, about 30 minutes. Pour off excess water. Keep warm.
3. While rice is about half-cooked, sauté the onions in 2 tablespoons butter until they turn just transparent. Add the chanterelles and apricots and continue to sauté for another 2 minutes.
4. Add salt and remaining 1 tablespoon butter and stir-fry for 1 minute.
5. Stir in the wild rice and blend until the rice is warmed and well-mixed with the mushrooms and apricots. Garnish with sumac.

SALAD OF MARINATED LACTARIOUS MUSHROOMS WITH ARUGULA

1 1/2 cups water
1/2 cup white wine vinegar
1/4 cup sugar
1 tablespoon kosher salt
1 tablespoon pickling spices
20 ounces lactarious mushrooms, blanched
2 bunches arugula

For the marinade:

1. Combine water, vinegar, sugar and salt in a pot. Bring to a boil, stirring to dissolve salt and sugar.
2. Let marinade simmer for 5 minutes.
3. Take marinade off heat and add spices
4. Add the mushrooms and let the marinade stand in the refrigerator for 24 hours.
5. Wash and dry arugula. Arrange a few arugula leaves on chilled plates and place mushrooms in center.

GRAND MARNIER SOUFFLÉ

6 eggs, separated
1/3 cup sugar
1/3 cup Grand Marnier
Sweet butter and sugar for coating soufflé dishes

1. In a large bowl, beat egg yolks and sugar until light and creamy. Mix in the Grand Marnier.
2. In another large bowl, beat the egg whites until they are stiff but not dry. Fold into the yolk mixture.
3. Butter and coat with sugar bottoms and sides of 4 individual soufflé dishes. Place on a baking sheet and fill each dish with the soufflé mixture.
4. Bake in a 400-degree oven for 7 minutes. Lower the temperature to 350 degrees and bake for 8 to 10 minutes. Serve at once.

In 1966, Julie Dannenbaum opened the Creative Cooking School in Philadelphia's Germantown. At that time, she had no idea her school would become the largest non-professional cooking school in the country. Her style and approach to cuisine are classic, yet her recipes are fresh and original.

Dannenbaum is the author of four cookbooks including *Fast and Fresh* and *Italian Fast and Fresh*. She teaches at The Greenbrier in West Virginia and at the Gritti Palace in Venice.

She and Kathleen Mulhern, proprietor of Harry's Bar and Grill, presented this dinner on March 22, 1985. The recipes are from *Italian Fast and Fresh*.

Harry's Bar and Grill is reminiscent of the atmosphere of a posh London club. The restaurant is located in the heart of Philadelphia's financial district. Its proprietor, Kathleen Mulhern, has created an establishment known for its prime steaks, carefully prepared pasta, and perfect martinis.

Fox and hound paintings surround the mahogany bar. Tables set with shaded candles create a warm and friendly atmosphere.

Specialties include Fettuccine Alfredo, Pasta of the Day, aged Prime Filet, Sirloin Strip with choice of sauces, Sautéed Calf's Liver, and a variety of veal. Harry's also presents a fresh grilled Fish of the Day along with shrimp and lobster dishes.

The bar features many fine wines by the glass and a list which boasts more than 20 California chardonnays.

JULIE'S LASAGNA BOLOGNESE

SAUTÉED FISH FILLETS WITH ROSEMARY

POTATOES

STEAMED SNOW PEAS

STRAWBERRIES AND RASPBERRIES
WITH ZABAGLIONE AND SHAVED CHOCOLATE

Pinot Grigio
Chianti
Serves 6

JULIE'S LASAGNA BOLOGNESE

For the Pasta:
8 fresh or packaged spinach lasagna noodles
For the Béchamel:
4 tablespoons butter
4 tablespoons flour
4 or more cups milk and cream seasoned with salt, pepper and nutmeg
For the Bolognese:
3 tablespoons butter
1 large onion, finely chopped
2 carrots, chopped
2 ribs celery, chopped
2 teaspoons finely chopped garlic
3/4 pound ground pork
3/4 pound ground beef (chuck)
1/2 teaspoon basil
1/2 teaspoon sage
1/2 teaspoon oregano
Pepper and pinch of freshly grated nutmeg
3 tablespoons butter
1 cup dry white wine
1 1/2 cups tomato puree
2 tablespoons tomato paste
1 1/2 cups chicken or beef stock
1 tablespoon butter
6 chicken livers
Salt and pepper to taste
1 cup heavy cream
Freshly grated Parmesan

1. Cook lasagna noodles according to directions on package and drain on a wet cloth so they do not stick together.
2. Melt the butter in a saucepan and add the flour. Stir to make a roux. Add the milk and cream with salt, pepper and nutmeg. Cook until thickened and set aside. This will yield a double batch of béchamel.
3. Melt the butter in a large sauté pan and add the onion, carrots, celery and garlic. In a mixing bowl combine the ground pork, ground beef, basil, sage, oregano, pepper and freshly grated nutmeg. In another large pan, melt butter and add meat mixture. Brown well. Add the vegetable mixture. Add dry white wine, tomato purée, tomato paste, chicken or beef stock.

4. Cover and cook for 1 hour (or until somewhat thickened). Stir occasionally. If it gets too thick add a little stock.
5. Melt butter in small pan and brown chicken livers on both sides, leaving centers pink. Chop finely and add to sauce in last 15 minutes of cooking. Add salt and pepper and heavy cream at the end of cooking.
6. Layer as for standard lasagna recipe, in a buttered ovenproof dish starting with pasta, meat sauce, pasta, béchamel, continue ending with layer of bechamel. Sprinkle with Parmesan and bake in a preheated 325-degree oven for 20 minutes or until top is brown and crispy.
7. Remove from oven and allow to rest for about 5 minutes before serving.

SAUTÉED FISH FILLETS

6 fish fillets
1/2 cup flour
3 tablespoons olive oil
3 tablespoons butter
Salt and fresh pepper to taste

1. Roll the fish fillets in flour and pat to remove excess.
2. Heat the oil and butter in a large sauté pan and when the foam subsides, add the fish fillets. Cook 3 to 4 minutes on each side. Season with salt and pepper.

ROSEMARY POTATOES

Olive oil
6 large potatoes, cut into chunks
3 fresh sprigs rosemary
Salt and pepper to taste

1. Spread some olive oil all over the bottom and sides of shallow pan. Add the potatoes. Drizzle olive oil over the potatoes. Add salt and pepper. Lay the rosemary sprigs on top of the potatoes.
2. Place in a preheated 450-degree oven and bake for 45 to 60 minutes, shaking the pan from time to time.

STRAWBERRIES AND RASPBERRIES WITH ZABAGLIONE AND SHAVED CHOCOLATE

For the Zabaglione:
3 eggs
3 egg yolks
2/3 cup sugar
1/4 cup sweet Marsala or any liqueur
2 pints strawberries
2 pints raspberries
Shaved bittersweet or white chocolate
1 cup heavy cream, whipped, optional

1. Put the eggs, egg yolks, sugar and Marsala into a zabaglione pot and beat with a whisk until blended. Hold the pot over high heat and continue beating; raise and lower the pot over the heat so that the pot never gets too hot. (Or put the ingredients into a large glass bowl, stand the bowl in a pan of hot water over high heat and beat with a whisk.)
2. When the zabaglione is thick and creamy (about 10 minutes over direct heat, 15 to 20 minutes over hot water), serve immediately in stem glasses or pour over fresh strawberries and raspberries.
3. If you wish to serve the zabaglione cold, whip 1 cup heavy cream until peaks form. Set the warm zabaglione over a bowl of ice and beat until finger warm. Fold the whipped cream into the mixture before pouring over berries.
4. Top with shaved bittersweet or white chocolate.

For a few weeks each year, Lorenza de' Medici, who traces her ancestry to Lorenzo de' Medici, offers Italian cooking classes at Badia a Coltibuono (Abbey of the Good Harvest), her eleventh century villa in Tuscany.

She is the author of many cookbooks, including *Recipes From the Badia*, 18 practical cooking manuals, and *Italy the Beautiful Cookbook*. She frequently gives demonstrations in Europe and America.

This meal was served at The Monte Carlo Living Room on March 26, 1987. All recipes are de' Medici's creations.

The Monte Carlo Living Room, is actually two restaurants in one. The formal dining room, resplendent with European furnishings and sparkling crystal, has an air of quiet elegance.

Chef Nunzio Patruno prepares dishes from the regions of Italy with a special emphasis on northern cuisine. Before the restaurant opened in 1982, Patruno studied throughout his native land and added a French touch to his art, working at the Polpetta in Monaco. Among his specialties are Ink Squid Pasta with Fresh Seafood, Broiled Sliced Polenta, Sweetbreads in Port, and Fresh Stuffed Artichokes.

Live entertainment and dancing are enjoyed on the second floor of this South Street restaurant, complete with cozy sofas and two bars. The Wednesday night happy hour offers a complimentary buffet and dancing into the night.

MENU

TUSCAN ANTIPASTO

(Antipasto Misto alla Toscana)

FILLET OF RED SNAPPER

(Pagelloa alla Livornese)

BEANS AND ARTICHOKES

(Fagioli e Carciofi)

GORGONZOLA AND ITALIAN FONTINA WITH FRESH PEARS

Coltibuono Bianco, 1985
Chianti Classico Riserva, 1979

Serves 6

TUSCAN ANTIPASTO
(Antipasto Misto alla Toscana)

Antipasto ingredients:
1 red pepper
1 yellow pepper
3 plum tomatoes
12 mushroom caps
6 French bread slices, toasted
1/2 pound chicken livers
To Prepare the Peppers:
2 anchovy fillets, finely chopped
1 tablespoon capers
1 tablespoon Parmesan cheese
1 tablespoon breadcrumbs
1 teaspoon chopped garlic
1 teaspoon chopped parsley
2 tablespoons olive oil
Salt and pepper

1. Slice the red pepper and the yellow pepper into 6 slices. Place in a pan and sprinkle evenly with anchovy fillets, capers, Parmesan cheese, breadcrumbs, chopped garlic, chopped parsley, olive oil, and salt and pepper.
2. Bake in a 350-degree oven for 15 minutes.

To Prepare the Tomatoes:
1 tablespoon Parmesan cheese
1 cup cooked spinach
1 whole egg
Salt and pepper
Pinch thyme

1. Slice tomatoes in half and scoop out the seeds. Mix Parmesan cheese, spinach, egg, salt, pepper, and thyme together and stuff the tomatoes with the mixture.
2. Bake in a 350-degree oven for 15 minutes.

To Prepare the Mushrooms:
1 tablespoon fresh minced garlic
1 tablespoon fresh chopped parsley
Olive oil for sprinkling
Salt and pepper to taste

1. Sprinkle mushrooms with fresh minced garlic, chopped parsley,

olive oil, salt and pepper. Broil or grill the mushrooms for 2 minutes.

For the Chicken Livers:
Olive oil for sautéeing the chicken livers
1 teaspoon finely minced shallots
1 teaspoon finely minced garlic
1/4 cup white wine
1 anchovy fillet, chopped
Pinch each of rosemary, thyme, and parsley
1 tablespoon capers

1. Heat the olive oil in a skillet and add the chicken livers. Sauté the chicken livers, mashing them with a wooden spoon. When the chicken livers begin to turn color, add remaining ingredients. Continue to sauté the mixture until it forms a chunky paste.
2. Top the French bread slices with chicken liver mixture.

To Serve the Antipasto:
Evenly distribute the antipasto on each of 6 serving plates.

FILLET OF RED SNAPPER
(Pagello alla Livornese)

6 tablespoons olive oil, approximately
2 cloves garlic, minced
6 fillets of red snapper (approximately 8 ounces each)
12 black olives
1 tablespoon capers
1/2 cup white wine
Salt and pepper to taste
1 pound fresh tomatoes, peeled, seeded and chopped
1 tablespoon unsalted butter
1 teaspoon fresh parsley, chopped
Pinch thyme

1. Heat a skillet and add olive oil and garlic. Sauté over medium heat. Do not allow garlic to burn. Add the fish and sauté about 1 minute on each side.
2. Add the olives, capers, white wine, salt, and pepper and sauté for 2 more minutes.
3. Remove fish from the pan, place on warm platter and cover with foil. Set aside.
4. Place the tomatoes, butter, parsley, and thyme in the pan. Bring to a gentle boil, lower the heat and simmer gently for 5 minutes or until sauce is completely heated through.
5. Spoon the sauce on top of the fish and decorate the platter with fresh basil and black olives.

BEANS AND ARTICHOKES *(Fagioli e Carciofi)*

1 cup white beans
4 scallions, finely chopped
6 plum tomatoes, roughly chopped
1/4 pound bacon, crisply fried and well-drained
3 tablespoons olive oil, divided
6 whole artichokes, cleaned, peeled and sliced
6 tablespoons chopped parsley
2 gloves garlic, finely minced
Salt and pepper to taste

1. Soak white beans in enough water to cover overnight.
2. Place the beans in a saucepan and add fresh scallions, tomatoes, bacon, 1 tablespoon olive oil, and salt and pepper to taste. Cook over medium heat until tender.
3. Meanwhile, in a sauté pan, add the remaining 2 tablespoons olive oil to the pan and add sliced artichokes, parsley, garlic, and salt and pepper. Sauté for 10 minutes.
4. Place the beans in a serving bowl. Place the artichokes on a serving platter.

Yamuna Devi (née Joan Campanella) was reared in Montana, far from India, whose cuisine she loves and has mastered. Devi, a devoted vegetarian, prepared meals for the late John Lennon, Indira Gandhi and several Maharajas. She now divides her time between her homes in England and Virginia where she lectures and gives cooking demonstrations. Her book, *Lord Krishna's Cuisine: The Art of Indian Vegetarian Cooking* was named best book of 1987 and best Asian cookbook by the International Association of Cooking Professionals.

The following dinner was served at The North Star Bar on March 20, 1988. All recipes are from *Lord Krishna's Cuisine*.

The North Star Bar is comprised of three rooms, each with its own feeling and atmosphere. Residents of the Fairmount neighborhood drop in for a beer, a chat with the bartender, and to watch the latest sports event on television.

Pure American fare and southwest dishes are served in the casual dining room, or patrons can elect to enjoy their burgers, pizza, nachos, or grilled steak in the airy atrium.

At 10:30 PM, the restaurant moves to the beat of The Daves, a local rock band, or the North Star may present other musical groups, poetry readings, or other entertainment.

MENU

**HERBED SPLIT PEA SOUP
WITH APPLE AND COCONUT**

(Masala Matar Dal)

**MIXED VEGETABLE FRITTERS
WITH FRESH CORIANDER CHUTNEY**

(Pakoras with Dhaniya Chatni)

**SWEET POTATO SALAD
IN MAPLE-LEMON VINAIGRETTE**

(Shakarkand Salaad)

FRESH FRUIT IN SEASON

Chateau Haut Caillou Sauvignon Blanc
Dopff au Moulin Gewürztraminer
Raymond Vineyards California Chardonnay

Serves 6

HERBED SPLIT PEA SOUP WITH APPLE AND COCONUT *(Masala Matar Dal)*

2/3 cup green or yellow split peas
1 teaspoon scraped, finely shredded or minced fresh ginger root
1 to 2 hot green chilies, minced
1 1/4 teaspoons cumin seeds
1 (2-inch) piece cinnamon stick
8 whole cloves
4 black peppercorns
4 tablespoons "ghee" (clarified unsalted butter) or vegetable oil
1 teaspoon tumeric
7 cups water
1 large cooking apple, cored and cut into 16 pieces
1/4 cup fresh or dried coconut
2 tablespoons minced fresh parsley or chopped coriander leaves
1 1/2 teaspoons salt

1. Soak the split peas in hot water for 5 hours. Drain.
2. Combine the ginger root, green chili, cumin seeds, cinnamon stick, cloves, and peppercorns in a small bowl. Heat the "ghee" or vegetable oil in a heavy 3-quart non-stick saucepan over moderate heat. When it is hot, sprinkle in the combined seasonings. Fry until the cumin seeds turn brown. Add the tumeric and follow immediately with the water.
3. Bring the liquid to a full boil and stir in the split peas, apple and coconut.
4. Reduce the heat to moderately low, cover and gently boil for 1 1/2 hours or until the "dal" is soft and fully cooked.

Remove from the heat and stir in the herb and salt. Then cover and allow the added seasonings to soak into the hot "dal" for 1 to 2 minutes. Stir and serve.

MIXED VEGETABLE FRITTERS
(Pakoras)

For the Pakoras Batter:
1 1/3 cups sifted chickpea flour (sifted before measuring)
2 teaspoons melted "ghee" (unsalted clarified butter) or vegetable oil
1 tablespoon lemon juice
1/4 teaspoon cayenne pepper
1/2 teaspoon tumeric
1 teaspoon "garam masala" (blend of powdered spices) or 1/4 teaspoon each ground cardamom, cumin, cinnamon and cloves with 2 teaspoons ground coriander
1 to 1 1/2 teaspoons salt
9 tablespoons cold water, or as needed
1/3 teaspoon baking powder (optional)
Pakora Suggestions:
Cauliflower florets, half-cooked
Eggplant, cut into 1/4-inch rounds
Spinach or Swiss chard leaves, bite-sized
Asparagus tips, blanched and dried
Potato or yam, peeled and cut into 1/8-inch rounds
Bell peppers, peeled, seeded and cut into 1/4-inch strips
Ghee or vegetable oil for deep-frying

1. Combine the flour, melted ghee or vegetable oil, lemon juice, spices, and salt in a bowl and mix well. Add 5 tablespoons water slowly, beating with an electric beater or wire whisk until the batter is smooth and free of lumps. Slowly add 3 tablespoons more water, continuing to beat until well mixed in consistency and if necessary, slowly add the remaining water until the batter resembles the consistency of heavy cream and easily coats a wooden spoon.
2. Alternately, place the batter ingredients in a food processor fitted with the metal blade or a blender, process until smooth, then transfer to a bowl. Cover the batter and set aside for 10 to 15 minutes.
3. Again beat with an electric beater, wire whisk or your hand for 2 to 3 minutes to further lighten the batter. (Check the batter consistency: if it is too thin, moist foods will spatter as they fry; if it is too thick, they will not cook properly. Add flour or water as necessary.) Stir in the baking powder at this time if you prefer a cake-like crust. Set all of the items to be fried next to the stove. They should be patted dry and at room temperature.

4. Heat 2 1/2 to 3 inches of fresh ghee or vegetable oil in a wok or deep frying pan until the temperature reaches 355 degrees. Dip 5 or 6 of your selected ingredients in the batter and, 1 at a time, carefully slip them into the hot oil. The temperature will fall but should then be maintained between 345 to 355 degrees throughout the frying. Fry until the pakoras are golden brown, turning to brown evenly. Leafy greens may take as little as 1 to 2 minutes per side, while potatoes may take up to 5 minutes per side.
5. Remove with a slotted spoon and drain on paper towels. Serve immediately or keep warm, uncovered, in a preheated 250-degree oven until all the pakoras are fried, up to 1/2 hour.

NOTE: It is convenient to keep a bowl of water and a tea towel near the frying area. After batter-dipping the items to be fried, rinse and dry your hands before continuing.

FRESH CORIANDER CHUTNEY
(Dhaniya Chatni)

1 teaspoon cumin seeds
3 tablespoons sesame seeds
1/4 cup freshly grated coconut or 1/4 cup chopped almonds
1 cup trimmed fresh coriander, slightly packed
1 to 2 hot chilies, seeded
1/2-inch piece peeled fresh ginger root, chopped
2 tablespoons water
1/4 cup sour cream or yogurt (optional)
1 tablespoon raw sugar or "jaggery" (raw cane sugar)
1 teaspoon salt

1. Combine the cumin seeds, sesame seeds and coconut or nuts in a heavy frying pan and place over low heat. Dry-roast, stirring frequently, until the coconut or nuts darken a few shades.
2. Combine the coconut mixture and the remaining ingredients in a food processor fitted with the metal blade, or in a blender. Process until smooth. (The texture should resemble runny apple-sauce; you may need more water to reach this consistency.) Transfer to a bowl and serve, or cover and keep refrigerated for about 2 days.

Makes 1 cup

SWEET POTATO SALAD IN MAPLE-LEMON VINAIGRETTE *(Shakarkand Salaad)*

6 medium-sized sweet potatoes (about 2 pounds), washed but not peeled
4 tablespoons maple syrup or honey
3 tablespoons orange or tangerine juice
3 tablespoons lemon or lime juice
3/4 teaspoon salt
1/4 teaspoon freshly ground black pepper or 1/8 teaspoon cayenne
1/2 cup olive oil, or 2 tablespoons almond oil or 6 tablespoons sunflower oil
1/3 cup finely chopped fresh coriander or parsley
2 tablespoons chopped candied or stem ginger
3 medium-sized tomatoes, peeled, seeded, cut into 1/2-inch cubes

1. Prick the potatoes with a fork in 2 or 3 places, then wrap in aluminum foil. Bake in a preheated 400-degree oven for about 45 minutes or just until crushably soft. Cool, peel, cut into 1/2-inch cubes and place them in a large salad bowl. Alternatively, peel the potatoes, steam them, let them cool and cube them.
2. Combine the sweetener, juices, salt, cayenne or black pepper, oil, fresh herbs and ginger in a jar, cover and shake until emulsified. Pour the dressing over the potatoes, toss gently, cover and refrigerate for 1 to 8 hours.
3. Before serving, add the tomatoes, gently toss and serve on a bed of mixed greens.

Although she calls Atlanta, Georgia home, Nathalie Dupree was born and raised in Trenton, New Jersey. Like so many transplanted northerners, Nathalie quickly adopted the warm southern style and true sense of hospitality which is the South's hallmark.

She is the host of "New Southern Cooking" on nationwide Public Television and author of the companion cookbook.

With the assistance of Judy DiVicaris and Bill Curry, proprietors of Cafe Nola, Dupree served this luncheon on March 18, 1988. All recipes are from *New Southern Cooking*.

Cafe Nola, with its special New Orleans cuisine and decor offered a natural kitchen to Dupree. Opened in 1980, Judy DiVicaris and Bill Curry decided to design a restaurant on colorful South Street, an area which reminded them of New Orleans. There's an oyster bar in the bar area, with a few tables and barstools where patrons enjoy a Cajun martini or oysters on the half shell.

Cafe Nola presents the best of New Orleans fare including Jambalaya, Crawfish Etouffé, Gumbo, and Shrimp Creole. The muffins and breads which accompany the meal are homemade and hard to resist. There's a fine selection of beer and wine to be enjoyed in a casual, but plush atmosphere.

HOT OR COLD SHRIMP PASTE (With Toast Points)

BILLY'S BAKED SHAD
WITH CORN BUTTER AND SAUTEED ROE

STEAMED, BUTTERED BROCCOLI FLORETS

LEMON CHESS PIE

Southern Iced Tea

Serves 6

HOT OR COLD SHRIMP PASTE
(With Toast Points)

1 cup butter
1 pound large shrimp, cooked and peeled (about 30-35 per pound)
Freshly grated nutmeg
Salt
Freshly ground black pepper
6 slices white bread toasted and cut into 4 triangles each

1. Preheat the oven to 350 degrees. In a bowl, whisk the butter until soft and white. Chop the shrimp fine in a food processor or blender and add to the butter, beating the mixture well. Season to taste with nutmeg, salt, and pepper.
2. Place in a buttered baking dish and bake 30 minutes or until the paste comes away from the sides of the baking dish and is light brown on top. Serve hot on toast points.

NOTE: This paste also can be served cold on toast points, sliced with cold meats, or hot like a quenelle.

BILLY'S BAKED SHAD WITH CORN BUTTER AND SAUTÉED ROE

For the Roe:
2 single roe, 6 to 8 ounces
Salt and freshly ground black pepper
8 tablespoons butter
2 tablespoons olive oil
For the Shad:
2 shad fillets, boned, 2 1/2 pounds each
2 cups flour
Salt and freshly ground black pepper
5 tablespoons butter, divided
Juice of 1 lemon
For the Corn Butter Sauce:
1 or 2 hot red peppers, seeded and chopped
5 tablespoons fresh corn off the cob
Juice of 2 limes
2 cups heavy cream
4 tablespoons butter
Salt and freshly ground black pepper

1. Preheat the oven to 400 degrees.
2. Season roe with salt and pepper. Heat the butter and oil to sizzling in a heavy pan and add the roe. Slash the roe with a knife a few times to prevent blistering. Turn down the heat to very low and let cook 5 minutes before turning. Remove to a warm plate when just pink inside.
3. To prepare shad, first remove the skin, then coat the shad in flour seasoned with salt and pepper. Melt 2 tablespoons of the butter and pour onto a long baking sheet. Place the shad on the sheet, dot with remaining 3 tablespoons butter, sprinkle with lemon juice. Bake 10 minutes per inch of thickness, about 7 minutes.
4. For the corn butter sauce, place the peppers and corn in the lime juice in a heavy pan and boil briefly until the juice is reduced by 1/2. Add the cream and butter and boil until the cream is reduced and thick. Taste and add salt and pepper if necessary.
5. Place the shad on a serving platter, surround with the sautéed roe and top with corn butter sauce.

LEMON CHESS PIE

For the Crust:
1 cup soft wheat flour
Salt
1/3 cup butter
3 to 4 tablespoons ice water
For the Filling:
2 cups sugar
1 tablespoon flour
1 tablespoon corn meal
3 eggs
4 tablespoons melted butter
1/4 cup milk
Juice and zest of 1 lemon
1 teaspoon vanilla

1. To make the crust, mix the flour and salt together in a bowl. Cut in the butter with a pastry blender or fork until the mixture resembles corn meal. Add the water, a little at a time, tossing with a pastry blender or fork until the mixture is moist and holds together easily. Cover with a damp cloth or plastic wrap and let rest a few minutes.
2. Flour a board or wax paper and roll out the pastry 1/8-inch thick or less, using a floured rolling pin. Place the pastry in a 9-inch pie pan. Trim the pastry 1 inch larger than the pie pan and make a decorative border by fluting the edge or folding under then pressing with the tines of a fork to create a pattern. Cover, place in freezer or chill for 30 minutes before baking.
3. Preheat the oven to 425 degrees. Crumble a piece of wax paper, then spread it out to the edges of the pan. Make a weight by filling the paper with raw rice or dried peas. Bake for 20 minutes. Carefully remove the paper with the rice or peas. Discard the paper, but save the rice or peas for the next time you prebake a pie crust.
4. To make the filling, toss the sugar together with the flour and corn meal. Add butter, milk, lemon juice, zest, and vanilla. Mix well. Preheat the oven to 350 degrees. Pour into the prebaked pie crust. Bake 30 minutes or until firm.

Makes 1 (9-inch) pie

Florence Fabricant is an expert food and wine matchmaker. She is on the staff at *The New York Times* and writes regularly for *Harper's Bazaar* and *Ms.* Her book, *Pleasures of the Table*, contains 35 menus for all occasions and is one of the first American cookbooks which matches wines to an entire meal.

She and Chef Karim Lakhani presented this meal at the Palace Hotel on March 18, 1989. All recipes are from *Pleasures of the Table*.

The Palace Hotel affords Philadelphia one of its most elegant dining rooms. Situated on the magisterial Benjamin Franklin Parkway, across the street from The Cathedral of SS. Peter and Paul, the Parkway is the city's complement to Paris' Champs Élysées. Sparkling crystal, fine china and linen provide diners with a continental setting which sets off the haute cuisine.

SPICED SHRIMP ORIENTAL

FILLET OF BEEF WITH PEPPERED ONION CONFIT

WILD RICE

MAPLE PECAN PIE

California Gewürztraminer
Red Burgundy
Serves 6

SPICED SHRIMP ORIENTAL

2 pounds medium shrimp, shelled and deveined
1 tablespoon salt
4 teaspoons vegetable oil, divided
1/2 tablespoon minced fresh ginger
1 small clove garlic, chopped
1 teaspoon minced fresh green chili pepper (canned jalapeño pepper can be substituted)
1 cup minced scallions
2 tablespoons Oriental sesame oil
2 tablespoons light soy sauce
2 tablespoons rice vinegar

1. Toss the shrimp with salt and set aside for 1 hour. Rinse thoroughly and pat dry. Salting shrimp is a Chinese technique that crisps and improves the texture.
2. Heat 1 teaspoon of vegetable oil in a wok or large skillet. Brush or swirl the oil to coat the pan. When the pan is very hot, add the shrimp and stir-fry gently, tossing the shrimp until they have turned pink and are beginning to char. Transfer shrimp to a bowl.
3. Add remaining 3 teaspoons of vegetable oil to the wok or skillet, lower heat and stir-fry ginger, garlic, chili peppers, and scallions for a minute or two. Pour these ingredients over the shrimp and mix.
4. Add the sesame oil, soy, and vinegar, stir to combine, and set aside at room temperature. Serve tepid or cooled.

FILLET OF BEEF WITH PEPPERED ONION CONFIT

1 whole fillet of beef, well trimmed and with the narrow end tied under, about 3 1/2 pounds
2 tablespoons vegetable oil
5 tablespoons sweet butter, divided
6 cups very thinly sliced onions
1/4 cup cognac
1/4 cup water
Freshly ground black pepper
Watercress for garnish, optional

1. Be sure the fillet is trimmed of as much fat as possible and that its silvery membrane has been peeled off. Tie the meat at 1-inch intervals with butcher's string. Cut the beef in half if you do not have a casserole large enough to hold it in one piece. Preheat the oven to 400 degrees.
2. Heat the oil in a casserole, and brown the meat on all sides over medium high heat. When the meat is browned, remove it from the casserole and set aside on a platter. Add 1 tablespoon of the butter and all of the onions to the casserole; cook the onions over very low heat until they are golden and tender. Stir in the cognac and water, scraping any bits up from the bottom of the casserole.
3. Return the meat to the casserole, setting it on the bed of onions. Cover and place the casserole in the oven. If you are braising the meat in one piece, time it for about 20 minutes for medium rare. If it was cut in two, it will require only 13 to 15 minutes. The best way to check for doneness is by using a small instant-read thermometer. For medium rare it should register 120 degrees.
4. Remove the meat from the casserole and allow to rest 10 minutes before carving. (It can rest longer.)
5. Return the casserole to the top of the stove and cook the onions over medium heat until the liquid has evaporated. Stir in the remaining 4 tablespoons butter and season liberally with freshly ground black pepper. If you wish to hold the meat, return it to the casserole and cover. It will keep warm, but not continue to cook for 20 to 30 minutes.
6. To serve, remove the string, cut the meat into 1/2-inch thick slices, and arrange them on a platter. Stir the onion confit to incorporate any juices released from the meat, reheat briefly, and spoon onto the platter, either in the center surrounded by the beef slices, or around the edges. Some watercress springs will add a touch of color. Serve immediately.

MAPLE PECAN PIE

1 recipe paté brisée for 9-inch tart pan or pie pan
1 cup pecan halves
3/4 cup dark corn syrup
3/4 cup pure maple syrup
4 tablespoons melted sweet butter
3 eggs, lightly beaten
1 teaspoon vanilla extract
1/2 cup chopped pecans
3/4 heavy cream, whipped

1. Preheat the oven to 425 degrees. Roll out pastry, line pie or tart pan, prick all over and line with foil. Weight it with dried beans or pastry weights. Bake for 6 to 8 minutes until the pastry looks dry but has not colored. Remove foil.
2. Remove pastry from oven and lower heat to 350 degrees. Spread pecan halves over pastry. Combine remaining ingredients, except the cream, and pour into the pie shell. Bake for 35 to 40 minutes, until filling is fairly firm. Cool and serve with whipped cream.

John D. Folse is a Cajun from St. James Parish located on the east bank of the Mississippi River between New Orleans and Baton Rouge. He and his wife Laulie own Lafitte's Landing Restaurant in Donaldsonville, Louisiana.

John Folse is recognized throughout the world as a master Cajun-Creole chef and is the author of *The Encyclopedia of Cajun & Creole Cuisine*. He prepared a special dinner for President Ronald Reagan and Soviet Premier Mikhail Gorbachev during the Moscow Summit in June, 1988. He and Chef Sam Talucci prepared this Sunday brunch on March 20, 1988 at Magnolia Cafe.

The Magnolia Cafe is a perfect spot for a power breakfast, casual lunch, full Cajun-Creole dinner, or after-theater supper. Located a few blocks from the Academy of Music and Shubert Theater, Magnolia Cafe features an extensive menu with the emphasis on the hot and spicy.

The restaurant has high ceilings and comfortable, light-wood furnishings. Owner Sam Talucci opened Magnolia Cafe three years ago. Authentic New Orleans dishes such as Chicken Big Mamou, Blackened Fish, Andouille Sausage, and Crawfish are featured along with less spicy fare such as the Grilled Fish of the Day and Poor Boy Sandwiches.

Magnolia Cafe features a fine wine list and a variety of domestic and imported beer.

PAN FRIED EGGPLANT WITH CRABMEAT

CHARBROILED BREAST OF MALLARD SALAD

CAJUN FETTUCCINE

ICE CREAM

Champagne

Serves 4

PAN FRIED EGGPLANT WITH CRABMEAT

1 cup vegetable oil
1 large eggplant, peeled and sliced 1/4-inch thick
1 cup egg wash
2 cups seasoned flour
4 ounces butter
1/4 cup chopped green onions
1 pound lump crabmeat
1 tablespoon lemon juice
Salt and pepper to taste
Hollandaise sauce

1. Place vegetable oil in heavy sauté pan over medium heat. Dip eggplant slices in egg wash and lightly coat with seasoned flour. Sauté until brown on first side. Turn slices over and cook approximately 2 minutes or until tender. Remove from pan and keep warm.
2. Place another sauté pan on medium high heat. Add butter and sauté green onions for 30 seconds. Add lump crabmeat, lemon juice, salt and pepper to taste.
3. Evenly divide eggplant slices among 4 serving plates. Top with crabmeat and Hollandaise sauce.

CHARBROILED BREAST OF MALLARD SALAD

1 egg yolk
2 tablespoons red wine vinegar
1 tablespoon chopped garlic
Zest and juice of 1 orange
1 teaspoon chopped parsley
1 teaspoon whole dried thyme
1/2 teaspoon dried tarragon leaves
1/4 teaspoon dried basil leaves
1/8 cup brandy
1 cup peanut or regular salad oil
1 tablespoon honey
1/2 teaspoon cracked black pepper
Salt and white pepper to taste
2 (4-ounce) duck breasts, skin removed, pounded to 1/8-inch thickness
1 head red leaf lettuce
1 head romaine lettuce
1 head iceberg lettuce
Orange slices, for garnish
Cherry tomatoes, for garnish

1. Place egg yolk in a small mixing bowl and add vinegar, garlic, zest and juice of the orange, parsley, thyme, tarragon, basil, and brandy. Whisk together well.
2. Add oil in a slow steady stream, whisking continuously until all is incorporated. Add cracked pepper, honey, salt and white pepper to taste. Place duck breasts in marinade at room temperature for 1 hour.
3. Grill over hot charcoal fire for about 1 1/2 to 2 minutes per side. Remove from fire and cool.
4. Clean lettuces, reserving 4 large romaine leaves for each plate, and mix together well.
5. Place 1 romaine leaf on each of 4 plates. Slice each cool duck breast into 10 slices. Put a handful of lettuce mixture on each romaine leaf. Put 1/2 of each duck breast (5 slices) on each salad. Ladle 3 to 4 ounces of the marinade over top. Garnish with orange slice and cherry tomatoes.

CAJUN FETTUCCINE

4 tablespoons butter
3 cloves chopped garlic
1/4 cup sliced mushrooms
1/4 cup whole chopped scallions
1 small tomato
4 ounces andouille or other higher quality smoked sausage, cut into 1/2-inch slices
4 ounces 50-count shrimp, peeled and deveined
1/2 ounce white wine
1 tablespoon lemon juice
1/4 cup heavy whipping cream
8 ounces lump crabmeat
1/4 cup chopped pimentoes
1 tablespoon chopped parsley
1/4 pound cold butter, chipped
Salt and cayenne pepper to taste
1 pound fettuccine, cooked when sauce is ready

1. In a heavy bottom sauce pan, melt butter over medium heat. Add garlic, mushrooms, scallions, tomato, and sausage. Sauté approximately 2 minutes. Add shrimp and continue to sauté over medium heat to render juices. Add white wine and lemon juice. Cook until shrimp are pink and firm and liquor has reduced to 4 tablespoons.
2. Add whipping cream and crabmeat and bring to a slight boil. Add pimentoes and parsley. Reduce heat to low.
3. Add chipped cold butter, 3 pieces at a time, swirling pan constantly. Do not use a spoon as hot spots will develop in the pan and butter solids and liquids will separate. This must be hand swirled. Continue until all butter has been added.
4. Season to taste, using salt and cayenne pepper. Place pasta in 4 serving plates and spoon sauce generously over pasta.

Pierre Franey comes from the village of St. Vinnemer in Burgundy, the land of "Coq au Vin," "Chevre de Bourgogne" and fine Chablis. His first kitchen chore was preparing hundreds of chestnuts for Christmas dinner.

In the 1950s, after an apprenticeship in France, Chef Pierre Franey found himself in the kitchen of New York's posh Le Pavillon. There he met Craig Claiborne who urged him to contribute to *The New York Times*. "The 60-Minute Gourmet," his popular column, runs every Wednesday. Pierre Franey is the author of eight cookbooks including two volumes of *60-Minute Gourmet*, and *The Seafood Cookbook: Classic to Contemporary*.

Franey and Kamol Phutlek, chef/proprietor of Alouette, created this dinner on March 18, 1988. All recipes are from *The Seafood Cookbook* which he coauthored with Bryan Miller. If there is such a thing as "Philadelphia Cuisine," Chef Kamol Phutlek may have invented it. The Thai-born chef found his way to Philadelphia during the early 70s and began to experiment, marrying French technique with American and Oriental ingredients. His restaurant, Alouette, situated in Queen Village, has exposed brick walls, candles, and a warm romantic atmosphere. The front room has a long bar and small tables in which to partake of an apéritif or a glass of wine from the international list. Alouette also features a fine list of vintage port and sherry, wines from California and around the world.

Phutlek's classic dishes include escargot, fresh fish, and fowl, usually accented with herbs, wine, or light cream. Desserts are unique, especially the White Chocolate Ice Cream with Raspberry Sauce.

MENU

CREAM OF MUSSEL SOUP WITH SAFFRON

CARPACCIO OF FRESH TUNA WITH GINGER-LIME DRESSING

SCALLOPS WITH ENDIVE

FRESH FRUIT IN SEASON

1983 Vouvray, Aigle Blanc P. Poniatowski
1982 Pinot Noir, Bouchaine, Napa Valley
Serves 4

CREAM OF MUSSEL SOUP WITH SAFFRON

3 tablespoons unsalted butter
4 tablespoons chopped shallots
4 tablespoons chopped onion
1 teaspoon chopped garlic
1/2 teaspoon saffron threads
2 quarts mussels, well scrubbed with beards removed
Tabasco sauce to taste
1/4 cup finely chopped fresh parsley leaves
1 1/2 cups dry white wine
2 cups heavy cream
1 cup light cream
Salt and freshly ground black pepper to taste

1. Melt butter in a soup pot over medium-high heat. Add the shallots, onion, garlic, and saffron. Cook, stirring, for about 3 minutes. Add the mussels, Tabasco sauce, parsley, and wine. Cover and cook until the mussels have opened, about 5 minutes.
2. Add the cream to the cooking liquid and bring to a boil. Season with salt and pepper. If necessary, keep warm over low heat.

CARPACCIO OF FRESH TUNA WITH GINGER-LIME DRESSING

4 tablespoons virgin olive oil plus oil to coat the plastic wrap
4 skinless trimmed tuna steaks, 3/8-inch thick (each about 4 1/2 ounces)
1 large egg yolk
1 tablespoon fresh lime juice
2 tablespoons heavy cream
1 teaspoon grated fresh ginger root
1/8 teaspoon minced garlic
1/2 teaspoon grated lime rind
1 1/2 teaspoons finely chopped chervil leaves, divided
1 1/2 teaspoons finely chopped fresh basil leaves, divided
Salt and freshly ground black pepper to taste

1. Brush 2 (10-inch) square sheets of plastic wrap with olive oil. Place 1 of the tuna steaks between the sheets of plastic wrap and place on a hard flat surface. Using a meat pounder or any flat-bottomed heavy implement, gently pound the tuna evenly into about a 1/8-inch-thick circle. Use a sharp knife or scissors to trim the ragged edges of the flattened fillet into a neat circle. Reserve the trimmings in the refrigerator.
2. Remove the top layer of plastic and lift the fillet onto an 8 to 10-inch-diameter chilled serving plate. Remove the top layer of plastic. Repeat this process with the remaining tuna steaks, placing 1 each on a chilled plate. Refrigerate the finished plates.
3. Make the dressing by putting the egg yolk in a bowl and whisking vigorously, add the lime juice as you whisk. Continue whisking and pour in a thin stream of oil. When the combination has thickened to mayonnaise consistency, gradually whip in the cream, ginger, garlic, lime rind, 1 teaspoon chervil, 1 teaspoon basil, and salt and pepper.
4. Season the fillets with pepper. Coat them with a thin layer of sauce. Remove the tuna trimmings from the refrigerator. Make decorative garnishes in the center of each plate by arranging the trimmings roughly into the shape of a rose (or any form desired).
5. Sprinkle remaining chervil and basil over each serving. Serve immediately.

SCALLOPS WITH ENDIVES

3/4 pound bay or sea scallops
2 large endives (about 1/2 pound total weight)
1 tablespoon unsalted butter
3 tablespoons finely chopped shallots
Juice of 1/2 lemon
1/2 cup dry white wine
1 cup heavy cream
1/2 teaspoon saffron threads, optional
1/8 teaspoon hot red pepper flakes
Salt and freshly ground black pepper to taste

1. If sea scallops are used, cut them into quarters. Set aside.
2. Trim off the ends of the endives. Cut the endives crosswise into 1-inch pieces. There should be about 4 cups loosely packed.
3. Melt the butter in a frying pan and add shallots. Cook briefly and add endives and lemon juice. Cook, stirring, until endives are wilted. Add wine and bring to a boil. Cover and simmer for 5 minutes.
4. Add 3/4 cup of the cream, saffron, hot pepper flakes and salt and pepper. Cook, uncovered over high heat, stirring often, for about 3 minutes.
5. Add the scallops and cook, stirring, for about 1 minute. Add remaining cream and salt and pepper to taste. Cook for about 2 minutes or until scallops have lost their raw look. Do not overcook. Serve immediately.

Barbara Gibbons is a nationally known syndicated columnist whose "Slim Gourmet" has attracted a loyal following. In a 1988 interview, Gibbons said she began to develop low calorie gourmet recipes when her daughter returned home from college carrying a few extra pounds.

Her numerous cookbooks, including *The International Slim Gourmet Cookbook* and *The Slim Gourmet Cookbook*, which won a Tastemaker Award, prove that tasty dishes don't have to be fattening.

Gibbons and Chef Edward Doherty created this dinner with recipes from *The International Slim Gourmet* at The London Restaurant & Bar on March 28, 1987.

The London Restaurant & Bar appeals to the sophisticated palate in an airy, relaxed atmosphere. Located in the city's Fairmount section, the bar dates back nearly 100 years when the London was a neighborhood tavern. The restaurant was renovated several years ago and includes two dining rooms appointed with blond wood furnishings, linen, and fresh flowers.

Chef Ed Doherty oversees the seasonal menu and selects the daily specials. On any given evening, the menu may feature Black Bean Soup, Carpaccio, Breast of Duck, Sweetbreads Wrapped in Breast of Chicken, and Tournedos of Beef. The restaurant also features a light fare menu of burgers, salads and stir-fry dishes. A fine wine list and domestic and imported beer are available.

The London presents a jazz trio or guitarist on the weekends in the bar area after the dinner hour.

MENU

BELGIUM ENDIVE, RADICCHIO, ARUGULA AND ENOKI MUSHROOMS IN A MISO AND LEMON DRESSING

CAPELLINI WITH PROSCUITTO, SUN-DRIED TOMATOES, ROASTED PEPPERS AND OYSTER MUSHROOMS IN A SEASONED VIRGIN OLIVE OIL

FRESH ITALIAN BREAD

RASPBERRY AND CHAMPAGNE SORBET

Chardonnay or Fumé Blanc

Serves 4

BELGIUM ENDIVE, RADICCHIO, ARUGULA AND ENOKI MUSHROOMS IN A MISO AND LEMON DRESSING

For the Salad:
2 heads Belgium endive
1 head radicchio
1 small bunch arugula
1/2 ounce fresh enoki mushrooms
For the Dressing:
2 tablespoons miso
2 tablespoons lemon juice
2 eggs
1 cup blended oil
1/4 teaspoon freshly ground black pepper

1. In a bowl, whisk together the miso, lemon juice, and the eggs. In a slow stream add the oil, stirring vigorously. Add pepper and adjust seasoning to taste.
2. Cut root stem from endive. Wash endive in cold water and pat dry with a paper towel. Separate radicchio into individual leaves. Wash and pat dry. Remove roots from arugula, wash and pat dry.
3. On 4 chilled salad plates, arrange the endive spears so that the root ends are touching in the center of the plate and the tips are evenly separated. The desired effect resembles a star.
4. Place the arugula in the center of the endive star.
5. Arrange the radicchio around the arugula.
6. Place a dollop of the dressing in the center of the salad.
7. Garnish with the enoki mushrooms on top of the dressing.

CAPELLINI WITH PROSCUITTO, SUN-DRIED TOMATOES, ROASTED PEPPERS AND OYSTER MUSHROOMS IN A SEASONED VIRGIN OLIVE OIL

1 red bell pepper
1 yellow pepper
1/2 cup blended oil (10% olive oil), divided
1/2 cup virgin olive oil
1 teaspoon fresh thyme leaves
1 bay leaf
Salt
1 pound capellini
2 ounces oyster mushrooms, sliced thin
4 ounces proscuitto, sliced very thin and julienned
4 ounces sun-dried tomatoes, julienned
Salt and black pepper to taste

1. Preheat the oven to 400 degrees. Rub peppers with blended oil and place in a heavy roasting pan. Cover with foil and bake until the peppers blister. Set aside and let cool.
2. In a heavy enamel sauce pan, heat olive oil, thyme, and bay leaf over medium heat for 10 minutes. Remove from heat and strain. Set aside.
3. Bring 6 quarts of cold water to a rapid boil with 1/4 cup blended oil and 2 tablespoons salt. Cook pasta 2 to 3 minutes, stirring constantly. Drain and refresh with cold water. Pour remaining blended oil in the palms of your hands. Work oil gently through the cooked pasta to prevent sticking.
4. Skin, seed and julienne peppers. In a large heavy enamel sauté pan, add reserved olive oil and mushrooms. Sauté over medium heat for 2 minutes. Add remaining ingredients and toss gently until heated through.
5. Garnish with fresh chopped parsley.

RASPBERRY AND CHAMPAGNE SORBET

2 cups raspberries
1/3 cup honey
1/2 cup champagne or dry sparkling wine

1. Purée raspberries in a food processor. In a sauce pan, combine honey and champagne. Simmer until honey is dissolved. Stir in raspberry purée.
2. Pour mixture into an 8-inch square pan and place in the freezer. Stir every 15 minutes until creamy. Cover and freeze until hard.
3. Scoop into cold dishes and garnish with mint leaves.

Libby Goldstein lives in the Queen Village section of Philadelphia where she tends her backyard garden and creates recipes with ingredients she grows.

She is President of the Food and Agriculture Task Force and wrote "The City Gardener," an urban cooking and gardening column, for the *Philadelphia Daily News*.

She and Jack McDavid, chef/proprietor of The Down Home Diner in the Reading Terminal Market, collaborated on this luncheon served on March 17, 1988.

Jack McDavid, the chef/owner of the Down Home Diner, wears a baseball cap which proclaims "Save the Farm." He calls his customers "ma'am" and "sir," and serves up fine southern cooking north of the Mason Dixon Line. When the Down Home Diner opened in the Reading Terminal Market, Philadelphians soon lined up for Fried Chicken, Sticky Buns, Hobo Stew, Homemade Biscuits, and Pan-Fried Catfish coated in pecans. The establishment is a nifty fifties throwback complete with neon signs, counter, booths, an old Coke machine, and Wurlitzer jukebox circa 1942.

McDavid, who once cooked lunch for Queen Elizabeth during his college days, makes everything from scratch including strawberry jam, ketchup, mayonnaise and pickled watermelon rind. He purchases his fish, fowl, and produce from Reading Terminal Market merchants, and these ingredients turn up in seasonal dishes prepared in American regional style, with the accent on the South.

SUPER SIMPLE SORREL SOUP

MOYER'S CROWN ROAST OF PORK GLAZED WITH HERB JELLY

HOMINY WITH GREENS AND PEPPERS

MOLASSES MINT ICE CREAM

Chaddsford Chardonnay

Serves 6

SUPER SIMPLE SORREL SOUP

1 to 2 handfuls sorrel leaves, about 4 to 8 ounces
3 tablespoons fresh chervil
2 pints chicken stock or canned chicken stock
2 tablespoons butter or bacon fat
Unflavored croutons

1. Remove stems and mid-ribs from sorrel and chop the leaves with the chervil.
2. Bring the stock to a boil in a non-aluminum pot and then lower the heat to a bare simmer.
3. Melt the butter or bacon fat in a skillet, add the chopped sorrel and chervil and stir them in the fat until they are quite wilted. Remove the wilted greens and add to the stock. Simmer for 5 minutes. Put the croutons in serving bowls and pour the soup over them.

MOYER'S CROWN ROAST OF PORK GLAZED WITH HERB JELLY

1 crown roast of pork or 1 (3-pound) boneless pork loin
For the Herb Jelly:
1 cup solidly packed herb leaves and stems, such as rosemary, tarragon and sage
1 1/4 cups cold water
1/2 cup herb vinegar
3 1/2 cups sugar
1 pouch liquid pectin

1. Steep the herbs in the water and vinegar in a covered glass or ceramic container for 1 to 2 days until the liquid smells and tastes of the herbs.
2. Strain the liquid into a 6-quart non-aluminum Dutch oven or preserving pan; add the sugar and dissolve without stirring.
3. When the sugar has dissolved, put the pot over high heat and, stirring all the while, bring to a full rolling boil; add the pectin.
4. Return to the boil for 30 seconds. Remove from the heat and skim off any foam.
5. Ladle into 3 to 4 hot, sterilized jars leaving 1/8-inch head space. Wipe the jar rims with a hot damp cloth, screw on canning lids that have been prepared according to manufacturer's directions and tighten. Process for 5 minutes in a boiling water bath.
6. Prepare your favorite crown roast of pork or boneless pork loin using the herb jelly as a glaze. Place about 1/2 cup water in roasting pan. Place glaze all over pork and baste every 15 minutes or so.

HOMINY WITH GREENS AND PEPPERS

2 pounds mustard greens, cut into thin strips or shredded
3 cups canned hominy or posole
3/4 cup liquid from the hominy can
3 tablespoons olive oil
2 cloves garlic, minced
2 fresh small hot peppers, seeded and cut into strips

1. Steam the mustard greens for 3 minutes and squeeze out any extra liquid by pressing them against the steamer with a wooden spoon.
2. In a saucepan, combine the greens, hominy and hominy liquid; simmer just long enough to heat the hominy.
3. In a small frying pan, heat the oil until it shivers; add the garlic and peppers. Sauté until the garlic starts to color.
4. Put the hominy and greens in a serving dish and pour the oil, garlic and peppers over them.

MOLASSES MINT ICE CREAM

1 handful fresh peppermint leaves and stems or 1 teaspoon peppermint extract
2 cups heavy cream
2 extra large eggs
3 ounces black strap molasses
1 ounce honey
1 1/4 cups light cream

1. Wash and blot the mint dry; place in a bowl and crush lightly. Add the heavy cream; cover the bowl and allow to steep in the refrigerator for 2 to 3 days. If you are using mint extract, omit this step.
2. Chill a 1 1/2-quart bowl, preferably metal, for 1/2 hour or more. Beat the eggs in the chilled bowl until thick and light. Little by little, add the molasses and honey, beating after each addition, until the mixture is very thick.
3. Strain the heavy cream into the bowl, squeezing the mint until all the cream is in the bowl. If using mint extract, beat it into the egg, molasses and honey mixture until well blended. Beat in the light cream.
4. Chill the mixture for 1/2 hour. Freeze according to ice cream maker's manufacturer's directions.
5. Serve with hot fudge sauce.

Makes 1 quart

The late Bert Greene was a writer, foodstuffs shopkeeper and columnist for *Chocolatier*. His love for cooking sprung from memories of his Queens, New York childhood during the Depression.

He was a cooking teacher who made many guest appearances on television, and the author of several cookbooks including *Greene on Greens* and *Kitchen Bouquets*. His last book, published posthumously, is *The Grains Cookbook*.

He created this special dinner at The White Dog Cafe on March 20, 1988. The soup recipe is from *Greene on Greens*. The spareribs and cake recipes are from *Kitchen Bouquets*.

The White Dog Cafe began as a tiny take-out muffin shop in University City. Today, proprietor Judy Wicks has turned the same townhouse, which was once home to the famous spiritualist Madame Blavatsky, into a restaurant famous for its innovative American cuisine of pure, direct, and earthy flavors.

Eight farmers from Pennsylvania raise and grow the ingredients Executive Chef Kevin von Klause uses to create his seasonal menu. The veal is humanely raised, the chickens are free range and so are the eggs used in cooking. Produce is organic and usually includes edible flowers, wild cress, baby greens, lovage, and red mustard leaves. Even the smoked pheasant sausage is homemade.

The White Dog Cafe has a friendly bar and live entertainment. Its decor features light wood furnishings, lace curtains, and knick knacks out of grandma's attic. The beer and wine offerings are extensive, and the restaurant offers many California wines.

CURRIED BUTTERNUT SQUASH BISQUE

FREETOWN SPARERIBS

FRENCH FRIED POTATOES

CORN ON THE COB

CHOCOLATE CUT VELVET

1985 Alderbrook Semillon

1984 Caymus Zinfandel

Serves 6

CURRIED BUTTERNUT SQUASH BISQUE

2 tablespoons unsalted butter
6 whole scallions, bulbs and green tops, finely chopped
1 clove garlic, minced
1 small green pepper, seeded, finely chopped
1/4 cup chopped fresh parsley, plus extra for garnish
2 teaspoons chopped fresh basil, or 1 teaspoon dried
1 (2-pound) butternut squash, peeled, seeded and cubed
1 ham bone, or 1/2-pound chunk of smoked ham
1 can (14-ounce) plum tomatoes
4 cups chicken broth
1/2 teaspoon ground allspice
1/4 teaspoon ground mace
Pinch freshly grated nutmeg
2 teaspoons curry powder
Salt and freshly ground black pepper

1. Melt the butter in a large saucepan over medium-low heat. Add the scallions; cook 2 minutes. Add the garlic, green pepper, 1/4 cup chopped parsley and basil. Cook, stirring occasionally, 5 minutes.
2. Add the squash to the saucepan. Toss to coat it with the scallion mixture. Add the ham bone or meat, tomatoes, broth, allspice, mace and nutmeg. Heat to a boil, reduce the heat. Simmer, covered, until the squash is very tender, about 1 hour. Remove the ham bone. (If ham meat was used, remove and save for use another time.)
3. Purée the soup in batches in a blender, being careful as hot liquid will expand. Transfer it to another large saucepan and stir in the curry powder. Heat to a boil; reduce the heat. Simmer 10 minutes, stirring frequently. Add salt and pepper to taste and sprinkle with parsley.

You may use an acorn squash for this recipe. Bake it cut-side down on a lightly buttered baking dish in a 350-degree oven for 45 minutes.

FREETOWN SPARERIBS

10 pounds spareribs
1 onion stuck with 2 cloves
1/4 cup soy sauce
2 teaspoons dried marjoram
1 teaspoon salt
1/2 teaspoon freshly ground pepper
2 tablespoons olive oil
2 yellow onions, finely chopped
2 cloves garlic, minced
1/2 teaspoon finely chopped fresh ginger
1 (17-ounce) can imported Italian tomatoes with juice, mashed
1 cup chili sauce
1/4 cup dark brown sugar
5 tablespoons honey
1/3 cup soy sauce
1/4 cup dry sherry
Pinch cayenne pepper
1 tablespoon chili powder
1/8 teaspoon dried oregano

1. Cut the ribs into 3-inch sections. Place in a large saucepan with water to cover. Add the onion with the cloves, 1/4 cup soy sauce, marjoram, salt, and pepper. Bring to a boil; reduce heat. Simmer 1 hour, turning the ribs once. Drain.
2. Meanwhile, heat the oil in a medium saucepan. Add the chopped onions, garlic, and ginger. Cook over low heat, stirring constantly, 5 minutes.
3. Add remaining ingredients, bring to a boil. Reduce heat. Simmer, stirring occasionally, 30 minutes. Heat oven to 350 degrees.
4. Using a sharp knife, cut rib sections into single portions and arrange in a single layer in a roasting pan or baking dish (pan must fit under broiler). Spoon sauce over and around ribs.
5. Bake 30 minutes, turning once and basting well with sauce. Place ribs under broiler until crisp; turn and broil other side until equally crisp.

NOTE: Spareribs may be prepared in advance before baking.

CHOCOLATE CUT VELVET

1 pound imported European sweet chocolate
1 tablespoon water
1 teaspoon vanilla
1 tablespoon all-purpose flour
1 tablespoon sugar
10 tablespoons butter, softened
4 eggs, separated
1 cup whipping cream
1 teaspoon Grand Marnier

1. Heat oven to 425 degrees. Heat the chocolate, water, and vanilla in the top of a 2-quart double boiler over low heat. Allow chocolate to melt very slowly. (It should take at least 10 minutes. Melting the chocolate too fast will turn it into a grainy lump.) Remove from heat. Stir in the flour, sugar, and butter.
2. Beat the egg yolks lightly. Whisk into the chocolate mixture.
3. Beat the egg whites until stiff but no dry peaks form. (Do not overbeat.) Fold gently into the chocolate mixture.
4. Line a buttered 8-inch springform pan with wax paper; butter the paper. Pour in the batter. Bake exactly 15 minutes. Turn off the heat and leave oven door ajar. Cool completely in the oven.
5. Carefully remove the outer rim of the cake pan. Place serving plate over cake and invert. Remove the wax paper (patience is a must here).
6. Whip the cream with the Grand Marnier until stiff. Using a pastry bag, pipe the cream over the top of the cake in a lattice pattern. Pipe stars around the base of the cake with the remaining cream. Refrigerate.
7. Remove cake from refrigerator 1/2 hour before serving. Cut into small pieces as it is rich.

NOTE: Do not use domestic chocolate; it just won't do!

Vertamae Grosvenor is an actress, novelist, poet, and good home cook. Although her travels take her around the world, her dishes are pure Southern soul food. Her commentaries are heard on National Public Radio's "All Things Considered." She is the author of *Vibration Cooking or The Travel Notes of a Geechee Girl*, which has been described as an autobiographical travelogue cookbook.

Grosvenor and Rosemarie Ritter prepared this authentic Southern dinner at Mama Rosa's on March 20, 1988. All recipes are from *Vibration Cooking*.

Mama Rosa's is the perfect place for an old fashioned Sunday dinner. The restaurant has a warm and homey atmosphere as tables are topped with red-checked cloths and meals are served family style.

Chef Rosemary Ritter oversees the menu which includes Southern favorites such as fried chicken, hot cornbread, smoky steamed collard greens, an assortment of salads, and sweet potato pie.

MENU

CHITTERLINGS A LA LARKINS

BLACKEYED PEAS A LA SANTA CLARA

COLE SLAW

POTATO SALAD

ICE CREAM

Lemonade

Serves 6

CHITTERLINGS A LA LARKINS

5 pounds (frozen) chitterlings
1 cup white wine vinegar
2 medium-size onions, divided
3 bay leaves
3 tablespoons soy sauce
1/2 teaspoon garlic powder or 3 cloves garlic (minced)
1 tablespoon Worcestershire sauce

1. Let chitterlings thaw completely, drain and clean. Place them in a bowl large enough to accommodate them and add 1 cup vinegar and 1 onion, cut up. Allow to marinate in the refrigerator overnight. This eliminates some of the odor so it won't be noticed during cooking.
2. Place the chitterlings in a large pot or Dutch oven. Add bay leaves, soy sauce, and garlic. Bring to a boil over medium heat and cook 1 1/2 to 2 hours or until tender. Do not add water. Remove chitterlings from the pot.
3. Cut them up into bite-size pieces and place in a large skillet. Add enough chitterling broth to cover. Dice the remaining onion and add to the skillet. Add the Worcestershire sauce and simmer 15 to 20 minutes.

BLACKEYED PEAS A LA SANTA CLARA

1 pound blackeyed peas
2 tablespoons butter
1 large chopped onion
3 to 4 cloves of garlic, minced
1 crushed dried hot red pepper
Salt
Cumin
Oregano
1 cup flour
1/2 teaspoon baking powder
1 egg
1/3 cup milk
1/4 cup fresh coriander

1. Soak the peas overnight. Rinse, drain and set aside.
2. In a heavy pot, melt the butter and sauté the onion, garlic, and hot pepper. Add salt, a touch of cumin, and oregano. Add the peas and water to cover and cook until tender.
3. In a bowl, mix flour, baking powder, egg, and milk. Add the fresh coriander. Blend well and drop by rounded spoonfuls onto the peas. Cover and cook for 15 minutes.

Chef Peter Grunauer began cooking in his parents' restaurant in Austria when he was ten years old. After he completed his culinary studies in Paris, Switzerland, and Germany, he came to New York where he developed "new Viennese cuisine." This light approach to Viennese fare was the hallmark of Vienna 79, Vienna Park and Fledermaus Cafe, Grunauer's New York City restaurants.

Grunauer is the co-author, with Andreas Kisler, of *New Viennese Cuisine: The New Approach*. During The Book and the Cook weekend of 1989, he and Chef Mario A. Musso prepared this classic yet modern Viennese dinner at the Hoffman House. All recipes are from *New Viennese Cuisine*.

The Hoffman House, located near the theater district, is an authentic German restaurant. Since it opened in 1923, it has been famous for classic German-Austrian cuisine including Weiner Schnitzel, Sauerbraten, and seasonal game, featuring venison and rabbit.

The bar and dining room are wood-paneled which adds to its middle European charm. Chef Mario A. Musso helped develop the present menu offering a variety of beef, fowl, and fish, including Poached Filet of Norwegian Salmon and Stuffed Quail. German side dishes such as Red Cabbage and Spatzle are also offered. Patrons end the meal with Warm Crepes and Sachertorte with Whipped Cream or other sweet classics.

The Hoffman House offers a wide selection of wine and imported beer.

CONSOMMÉ WITH LIVER DUMPLINGS

(Leberknödelsuppe)

FILET OF LEMON SOLE WITH LEEK CREAM

(Filets von Seezungen in Zitronen Lauch Creme)

FRESH STEAMED SPINACH

CHOCOLATE LAYER CAKE WITH WHIPPED CREAM

(Sachertorte mit Schlag)

Grinzinger Chardonnay

Serves 6

CONSOMMÉ WITH LIVER DUMPLINGS
(Leberknödelsuppe)

For the Cold Bouillon:
2 pounds beef bones, cut into 3-inch pieces
2 medium onions, unpeeled
5 quarts cold water
1 1/2 pounds beef, rinsed under cold water
1/2 leek, well washed and trimmed
1/4 celery root (celeriac), peeled
2 medium carrots, peeled
1 clove garlic, peeled
Stems of 1 bunch parsley, rinsed
10 black peppercorns
1 bay leaf
Salt to taste
For the Consommé:
1 pound lean ground beef
1 medium carrot, peeled and finely diced
1/4 celery root (celeriac), peeled and finely diced
1/2 bunch parsley, finely chopped
3 egg whites
6 black peppercorns
2 quarts cold bouillon
Salt to taste
For the Liver Dumplings:
1/2 pound calf's liver, with skin and sinews removed
1/2 cup chopped bacon
3 French rolls, soaked in 1/2 cup milk, with all the liquid then squeezed out
1 medium onion, thinly sliced
1 tablespoon salad oil
2 eggs
1 clove garlic, peeled and finely chopped
1/2 bunch parsley, finely chopped
1/4 teaspoon dried marjoram
Salt and freshly ground white pepper to taste
1/2 cup bread crumbs
4 cups bouillon

1. To make the bouillon, rinse the beef bones under cold water, blanch them in boiling water for 2 minutes, then rinse again in cold water.
2. Cut the unpeeled onions in half. Place the cut sides down on a hot stove burner or over a low flame and allow to char.

3. Place the blanched bones and the beef in a large pot with 5 quarts cold water. Bring to a boil, lower the heat and simmer, uncovered, for 2 hours, skimming frequently. Remove the meat.
4. Add the charred onions, leek, celery root, carrots, garlic, parsley stems, peppercorns, bay leaf and salt to taste. Cover and continue simmering for another 2 hours.
5. Strain the bouillon first through a sieve and then through cheesecloth. Discard meat and vegetables.
6. Refrigerate overnight and skim again for the clearest possible bouillon.
7. To make the consommé, mix ground beef, vegetables, egg whites and enough water so that the mixture is still thick but holds together. Refrigerate for 3 hours.
8. Place this mixture in a pot with the peppercorns. Add the cold bouillon. Bring to a boil, stirring frequently. When the boiling point has been reached, stop stirring and allow grease to rise to the surface. Simmer the soup for 1 1/2 hours, skimming occasionally.
9. Strain through cheesecloth, discard the solids, season with salt and bring quickly to a boil.
10. To make the liver dumplings, grind the liver, bacon and soaked rolls together. (You can use a food processor.)
11. In a skillet, fry the onion in the oil over medium-high heat until translucent, about 10 minutes.
12. In a large bowl, mix the ground liver mixture with the eggs, onion, garlic and parsley.
13. Season with the marjoram, and salt and pepper to taste. Thicken with the bread crumbs and form balls of equal size (about 8 to 10).
14. In a saucepan, bring the bouillon to a boil, add the dumplings, reduce the heat and simmer for 10 minutes.
15. Remove the dumplings and serve afloat in the consommé.

FILET OF LEMON SOLE WITH A LEEK CREAM

(Filets von Seezungen in Zitronen Lauch Creme)

1/2 cup plus 2 tablespoons clarified butter, divided
3 leeks (white portion only), rinsed thoroughly; 2 thinly sliced, and 1 thinly sliced lengthwise a la julienne and kept separately from the other 2
6 shallots, peeled and finely diced
1/3 cup fish stock
1/4 cup dry vermouth
1/4 cup dry white wine
1 cup heavy cream
Juice of 1 lemon
Salt and freshly ground white pepper to taste
6 (6-ounce) lemon sole fillets
Flour for the fish

1. Heat 1/4 cup of the clarified butter in a skillet over low heat. Add the 2 sliced leeks and allow to sweat.
2. Add the shallots and continue cooking until transparent.
3. Add the fish stock, vermouth and white wine. Bring to a very slow boil. Overcook the leek to make sure it is quite soft. This should take about 10 minutes. When the leek is soft, allow the mixture to cool and purée in a blender to a smooth consistency.
4. Transfer the mixture to a saucepan. Add the cream and stir constantly over medium heat until reduced to a sauce consistency. Stir in the lemon juice, and season with salt and pepper to taste. Set aside.
5. Dip one side of each lemon sole fillet in flour and shake off the excess. Heat 1/4 cup of the clarified butter in a large skillet over medium-high heat. Fry the fish first on the floured side until golden, then turn and fry on the other side until golden outside and slightly pink inside. Remove and keep the fish warm on a covered plate.
6. Add 2 tablespoons clarified butter to the skillet and sauté the julienned leek over medium heat for 3 to 4 minutes. Add a few tablespoons of water and allow the leek to blanch.
7. Pour the sauce on 6 warm plates. Arrange the fish over the sauce and garnish with the julienned leek.

CHOCOLATE LAYER CAKE WITH WHIPPED CREAM
(Sachertorte mit Schlag)

9 tablespoons unsalted butter
1/2 cup powdered sugar
6 eggs, separated, at room temperature
1 teaspoon vanilla extract
4 1/2 ounces dark sweet chocolate
1/4 teaspoon salt
1/2 cup granulated sugar
1/2 cup plus 1 tablespoon sifted flour
1 cup apricot jam
For the Glaze:
1 1/4 cups granulated sugar
9 ounces sweet chocolate
Whipped cream

1. Preheat the oven to 400 degrees. In a large bowl, cream the butter and the powdered sugar with an electric mixer. Beat in the egg yolks and the vanilla.
2. Melt the dark chocolate in a double boiler. With the electric mixer, beat the melted chocolate into the butter-sugar-egg yolk mixture.
3. Beat the egg whites, salt and granulated sugar to a stiff meringue. Slowly and carefully fold the meringue into the chocolate mixture. Resift the flour over the meringue mixture and gently fold in.
4. Cover the bottom and sides of a 10-inch springform cake pan with baking parchment. Pour in the cake mixture and bake for 45 minutes. Remove from the oven. Run a knife around the edge of the pan, reverse and unmold onto a wire rack. Allow to cool.
5. When the cake has cooled, cut into 2 equal layers. Spread half of the apricot jam over one layer, cover with the other and spread the rest of the jam over the top.
6. To make the glaze, place the sugar, 1/2 cup plus 1 tablespoon cold water, and the sweet chocolate in a pan over medium heat. Stir constantly until the sugar and chocolate have melted. Bring the glaze to 200 degrees on a candy thermometer. Remove from the flame, stir with a spatula until smooth and immediately pour over the top of the cake. The glaze will run down to cover the sides of the cake.
7. Let cool, slice and serve with freshly whipped cream.

Although Jessica B. Harris holds a doctorate in performance studies from New York University and teaches college level English and French, she is well-known for her food and travel articles. Her work has appeared in *Travel Weekly*, *Vogue*, and she was the "Go Gourmet" columnist for *Essence*. Her book, *Hot Stuff: A Cookbook in Praise of the Piquant* is a journey through 35 countries whose cuisines center on the hot and spicy. The recipes were collected in their country of origin.

This brunch was prepared at Copa, Too! on March 29, 1987. The recipes for the salad and plantains are from *Hot Stuff*. Chef Tom Petersen adapted the recipe for the grilled shrimp from Harris' book.

Copa, Too! is a bi-level casual restaurant located near the Academy of Music and the Shubert Theater. It has a comfortable bar, light furniture, and a big screen cable television for those who enjoy watching the Phillies, Flyers, Sixers or Eagles.

It specializes in fun food and drink from faraway places. With the help of Tom Petersen, owners Judy DiVicaris and Bill Curry have created a menu of Caribbean and Tex-Mex fare. Copaburgers with choice of topping, nachos and guacamole, Mexican Chicken or Beef Fajitas (all washed down with fresh lime margaritas) are a few choices at Copa, Too!

SPICED SUMMER FRUIT SALAD (Malaysia)

GRILLED SHRIMP WITH LIME AND CILANTRO (United States)

FRIED PLANTAIN (Puerto Rico)

Tropical Rum Punch

Serves 6

SPICED SUMMER FRUIT SALAD (Malaysia)

1 medium-sized firm mango, peeled and cut into 1/2-inch dice
2 medium-sized crisp Granny Smith apples, peeled, cored and cut into 1/2-inch dice
1/2 fresh pineapple, cut into 1/2-inch dice
1 large pink grapefruit, peeled and divided into segments, with the membrane removed
1 large orange, peeled and divided into segments
1/2 teaspoon Asian chile powder (this type has no cumin), available at gourmet shops or Mexican food stores
1/4 cup natural raw or dark brown sugar
1 tablespoon orange water (be sure that the orange water you purchase is suitable for internal use), available at gourmet shops.
Salt to taste

1. Place the fruit in a nonreactive glass or ceramic bowl. Let the fruit salad stand so the juices will mingle.
2. Meanwhile, in a small bowl, mix the chile powder, sugar, orange water and salt. Add to the fruit and mix it well with the juices that have drained.
3. Cover the bowl with plastic wrap and refrigerate it for at least half an hour to allow the flavor to develop. Serve chilled.

GRILLED SHRIMP WITH LIME AND CILANTRO (United States)

1 cup pure olive oil
1 cup peanut oil
2 jalapeño peppers, deveined and deseeded, diced very finely
1 teaspoon dried crushed hot red chile
2 tablespoons fresh cilantro, chopped
1 cup lime juice, freshly squeezed
Salt and pepper to taste
1 red bell pepper, deseeded and cut into 1-inch pieces
1 green bell pepper, deseeded and cut into 1-inch pieces
1/2 medium pineapple, cored and cut into triangles, leaving skin on.
36 jumbo shrimp

1. In a glass or ceramic bowl, combine the olive oil, peanut oil, jalapeño peppers, crushed red chile, cilantro and lime juice. Add salt and pepper to taste. Mix well and add the cleaned shrimp to the marinade. Cover and refrigerate overnight (the shrimp should be marinated overnight to allow the flavors to blend).
2. Heat the outdoor grill to cooking temperature. Meanwhile, place the shrimp, bell peppers and pineapple on metal skewers alternating items for color and taste contrast.
3. Cook approximately 5 minutes per side, basting with the marinade. Be careful of the flames caused by the marinade hitting the coals. May be served "as is" or on a bed of rice or pasta.

NOTE: Shrimp may be grilled in an oven broiler.

FRIED PLANTAIN (Puerto Rico)

2 pounds ripe plantains
2 cups vegetable oil for frying
1 tablespoon sugar

1. Peel the plantains and slice them lengthwise. Heat the oil in a heavy frying pan and fry the plantain slices for 5 minutes on each side, or until they are brown and crisp on the outside.
2. Sprinkle sugar over the slices and serve hot.

If America has a "First Lady of Desserts," she is certainly Maida Heatter. Some of her recipes are family heirlooms, others she has picked up during her many travels. Many are Heatter originals. Maida Heatter has written several "sweet" books including *Maida Heatter's Book of Great Desserts* and *Maida Heatter's Book of Great American Desserts*.

On March 28, 1987, Heatter's desserts were featured at a tea dance in the Swann Lounge at the Four Seasons Hotel. The recipes for the brownies and the cookies can be found in *Great American Desserts*. The cake recipe is from *Great Desserts*.

Philadelphia's Four Seasons Hotel overlooks the Benjamin Franklin Parkway near Logan Circle. It has two restaurants, each with its own menu and atmosphere.

People gather in the Swann Lounge for lunch, afternoon tea, a light bite, and after-theater desserts and coffee. The room is appointed with comfortable sofas, easy chairs, and a bar. Pasta, salads, and sandwiches are served through lunch; but at teatime, the room takes on a more quiet air. Cucumber sandwiches, miniature fruit tarts, and choice of teas are enjoyed until the first patrons arrive for the cocktail hour. During the weekend, the Swann Lounge toasts Vienna with an elaborate dessert table laid with pastries, cakes, and a choice of coffees.

The Fountain is the hotel's formal restaurant which serves both a prix fixe dinner and a menu a la carte. The rooms have dark wood panels, crisp white linen, silver candlesticks, and mounds of fresh flowers. Executive Chef Jean-Marie Lacroix keeps a close eye on his talented staff. The menu is international and features fresh fish in season; breast of Peking duck, which is a specialty; and prime beef. The wine list contains many of the world's finest vintages.

KATHARINE HEPBURN'S RASPBERRY BROWNIES

AMERICAN CHOCOLATE LAYER CAKE

GRANNY'S OLD FASHION SUGAR COOKIES

Darjeerling and Jasmine Tea

Serves 16 to 20

KATHARINE HEPBURN'S RASPBERRY BROWNIES

2 ounces unsweetened chocolate
4 ounces (1 stick) unsalted butter
1/4 teaspoon salt
1/2 teaspoon vanilla extract
1 cup granulated sugar
2 eggs graded "large"
1/4 cup unsifted all-purpose flour
4 ounces (generous cup) walnuts, broken into pieces
1/3 cup seedless red raspberry preserves

1. (Do not preheat the oven now.) Prepare an 8 x 2-inch square cake pan as follows. Turn the pan over, center a 12-inch square of aluminum foil over the pan, fold down the sides and corners to shape the foil, then remove it, turn the pan over again, place the foil in the pan and press it gently into place. Brush the foil all over with melted butter (additional to that called for) or spread the butter with crumpled wax paper and set the pan aside.
2. Place the chocolate and butter in a large, heavy saucepan over low heat. Stir frequently until melted. Remove the pan from heat, stir in salt, vanilla, sugar, and then the eggs 1 at a time, stirring until incorporated after each addition. Add the flour and stir briskly with a rubber or wooden spatula until smooth. Then stir in the nuts.
3. You will have about 2 1/2 cups batter. Pour half of it (about 1 1/4 cups) into the prepared pan. Tilt the pan to level the mixture or spread it with the bottom of a spoon.
4. Place the pan in the freezer for about 30 minutes or longer until the mixture is just firm enough for you to spread a thin layer of preserves on top.
5. Spread the preserves all over the top; it will be a very thin layer - barely enough to cover the brownie mixture.
6. Now pour or spoon small amounts at a time of the remaining brownie mixture over the preserves and smooth with the back of a spoon.
7. Let stand at room temperature for at least 30 minutes (or longer) until the frozen layer has thawed.
8. Meanwhile, adjust a rack 1/3 up from the bottom of the oven and preheat the oven to 325 degrees.
9. Bake for 40 minutes or until a toothpick inserted gently in the middle comes out barely clean.

10. Let stand in the pan until the cake reaches room temperature. Then place the pan in the freezer until the cake is firm. Cover with a small cutting board or cookie sheet, turn the pan and board or sheet over, remove the pan, peel off the foil and with your hands turn the cake right side up.
11. With a long, thin, sharp knife, cut the brownies into 16 squares or 32 small finger-shaped pieces. Serve at room temperature, cold, or very cold (almost frozen).

NOTE: Heatter says "This is one of the best brownies ever. It is Katharine Hepburn's marvelous recipe . . . to which I have added a thin layer of raspberry preserves in the middle before baking. If they gave Oscars for brownies, this would win."

GRANNY'S OLD-FASHIONED SUGAR COOKIES

1 3/4 cups unsifted all-purpose flour
2 teaspoons double-acting baking powder
1/4 teaspoon salt
4 ounces (1 stick) unsalted butter
Finely grated rind of 2 lemons
1 tablespoon lemon juice
1 cup granulated sugar
1 egg graded "large"
2 tablespoons whipping cream

1. Sift together the flour, baking powder, and salt and set aside.
2. In the large bowl of an electric mixer beat the butter until soft. Beat in the lemon rind and juice, and then add the sugar. Beat in the egg and the whipping cream. Then, on low speed, gradually add the sifted dry ingredients and beat until smoothly mixed. Remove from the mixer.
3. Turn the dough out onto a length of wax paper or plastic wrap, wrap it and refrigerate overnight. (In a hurry, I have used the freezer instead of the refrigerator - only until the dough was cold and firm but not frozen.)
4. When you are ready to bake, adjust 2 racks to divide the oven into thirds and preheat to 375 degrees. Line cookie sheets with baking pan liner paper or with foil shiny side up. Set aside.
5. Spread out a pastry cloth, flour it well and flour a rolling pin. Unwrap the dough, cut it into thirds and place 1 piece on the floured cloth. If it was refrigerated overnight, it will be too stiff to roll out; pound it firmly with the floured rolling pin, turning the dough over occasionally until it is soft enough to be rolled. Roll it out until it is quite thin, about 1/8 to 3/16-inch thick.
6. Use a large round cookie cutter about 3 1/2 inches in diameter (more or less). Start to cut the cookies at the outside edge of the dough and cut them so close to each other that they are touching. With a wide metal spatula transfer the cookies to the lined sheets, placing them 1/2-inch apart.
7. It is best not to reroll the scraps if possible because they would absorb additional flour and would become a bit tougher than otherwise. Here's a hint: Do not press the scraps together but, with smaller cutters, cut out as many smaller cookies as you can, or use a knife and cut squares or triangles. There will still be some leftover scraps, but much less than otherwise. Reserve the scraps. Roll and cut the remaining dough. Then press all the scraps together, refrigerate if necessary (it probably will not be), roll it out and cut with a knife or cutter.

Cinnamon-Sugar:
1 tablespoon granulated sugar
1/3 teaspoon cinnamon

1. Mix the above ingredients and, with your fingertips, sprinkle over the cookies.
2. Bake for 10 to 13 minutes, reversing the sheets top to bottom and front to back as necessary to ensure even browning.
3. When done, the cookies will be only sandy colored, slightly darker on the rims.
4. With a wide spatula, transfer the cookies to racks to cool. Store airtight. These will last well if you stay away from them.

   Makes 18 to 24 large cookies

AMERICAN CHOCOLATE LAYER CAKE

For the Cake:
4 cups sifted all-purpose flour
4 teaspoons double-acting baking powder
1/4 teaspoon baking soda
1/2 teaspoon salt
1 pound (4 sticks) unsalted butter
1 1/2 teaspoons vanilla extract
1/2 teaspoon almond extract
2 cups granulated sugar
6 eggs graded "large"
3/4 cup milk
6 ounces (1 1/2 cups) walnuts, cut or broken into medium-size pieces, optional
For the Icing:
16 ounces milk chocolate
12 ounces semisweet chocolate (I use 1-ounce squares of Hershey or Nestle; use any semisweet you like)
Pinch of salt
1 teaspoon vanilla extract
1 pint (2 cups) sour cream

1. Adjust 2 racks to divide the oven into thirds and preheat the oven to 350 degrees. Butter 4 (9-inch) round layer cake pans, line them with baking pan liner paper or wax paper cut to fit, butter the paper, dust the pans all over with fine dry bread crumbs, tilt the pans from side to side to coat them evenly, and then turn them upside down over paper and tap them to shake out loose crumbs. Set the pans aside.
2. Sift together the flour, baking powder, baking soda, and salt and set aside.
3. In the large bowl of an electric mixer beat the butter until soft. Add the vanilla and almond extracts and then the sugar and beat to mix. Add the eggs 1 or 2 at a time, and beat until incorporated after each addition. On low speed add the sifted dry ingredients in 3 additions, alternating with the milk in 2 additions.
4. Remove the bowl from the mixer. You will have a generous 8 cups of batter. Place a generous 2 cups in 2 of the prepared pans. Stir the optional nuts into the remaining batter and place 1/2 of it (a generous 2 cups) in each of the 2 remaining pans.
5. With the underside of a large spoon spread the batter to the sides of the pans. To encourage the cakes to rise with flat tops (without domes) spread the batter more thickly around the edges and slightly thinner in the middle of the pans.

6. Place 2 of the pans on each oven rack, staggering them so that the pans on the lower rack are not directly below those above.
7. Bake for 25 to 28 minutes. (I have made this cake many times and have never found it necessary to change the positions of the pans during baking; somehow they always bake evenly, even though that is unusual for my oven.) Bake until the tops just barely spring back when they are gently pressed with a fingertip, and the sides of the cakes just barely begin to come away from the sides of the pans. Do not overbake or the cake will be dry.
8. As soon as the cakes are done remove them from the oven, cover each one with a rack and turn the pan and rack over, remove the pan - cover with another rack and invert again, leaving the cakes right side up again. Brush each cake with a pastry brush to remove loose crumbs on the sides.
9. Prepare a large flat cake plate by lining it with 4 strips of wax paper. Place 1 cake on the plate, checking to be sure that it touches the papers all around. If you have a cake-decorating turntable, place the cake plate on it.
10. Let stand, and make the icing. Or, if you wish, the icing may be made while the cakes are baking.
11. Break up the chocolates and place them in the top of a large double boiler over shallow warm water on low heat. Cover the pot with a folded paper towel (to absorb steam) and with the pot cover. Let cook until almost completely melted, then uncover and stir with a wooden spatula until completely melted.
12. Transfer to the large bowl of an electric mixer. Add the salt, vanilla, and sour cream and beat on low speed until as smooth as satin (this is spectacular looking).
13. Let stand at room temperature for about an hour or so until cool and slightly thickened.
14. If you have a cake-decorating turntable and are experienced at using it you will probably want to smooth the icing on top and sides; without a turntable you will probably want to form the icing into swirls. If you plan to smooth it, you will probably also want to form a circle of rosettes around the top rim. If so, remove and reserve about 2/3 cup of the icing.
15. Whether you plan to smooth the icing or swirl it, do not use too much between the layers or you will not have enough to go around (in spite of the fact that this looks like enough icing for a dozen cakes).
16. With a long, narrow metal spatula spread a scant 1/4-inch layer of icing over the cake, making it a bit thicker at the rim to fill in the space. Place the next layer on (if you have used nuts, alternate the nut layers with the plain ones) right side up and ice the same as you did the first. Place the third layer on, right side up (align the layers carefully), ice and then place the fourth layer on, right side up (all four layers are right side up).

17. Cover the sides of the cake with the icing and then the top. Make sure it is all straight and even. Then smooth or swirl. Carefully remove the paper strips by slowly pulling each one out toward a narrow end.
18. If you have smoothed the icing and if you would like to decorate the rim (I do), fit a 12-inch pastry bag with a star-shaped tube. Fold down the sides of the bag toward the outside to make a 2 or 3-inch hem, transfer the reserved icing to the pastry bag, unfold the hem and twist the top of the bag closed.
19. If you are working on a counter top transfer the cake and the turntable to a table; it is easier to use a pastry bag for decorating the top of a cake if you are working above it rather than alongside it - especially a cake this high. Form a row of rather large rosettes (about the size of Hershey's Kisses) just touching one another on top of the cake around the rim.

Serve on wide plates.

Ken Hom lives in Berkeley, California and Paris. As a master Chinese chef, Hom decided to marry French culinary technique with Oriental ingredients. The result is "Chinoise Francais," a new cuisine which has become popular with Chinese food enthusiasts in the United States.

He was the host of "Ken Hom's Chinese Cookery" on Public Television and is the author of *Chinese Technique*, the companion cookbook to the series. His other books include *Ken Hom's East Meets West Cuisine* and *Fragrant Harbor Tastes: The New Chinese Cooking of Hong Kong*.

Hom prepared this dinner with Chef Derek Davis at the 1701 Cafe in the Warwick Hotel on March 19, 1989. The recipes for the soup and chicken are from *East Meets West Cuisine*. The recipe for the dessert is from *Fragrant Harbor Tastes: The New Chinese Cooking of Hong Kong*.

The Warwick Hotel is one block from Rittenhouse Square. One of its restaurants, the 1701 Cafe, has dark wood paneled walls with sconces that give a soft light to the dining room. White clothed tables and comfortable seating make the 1701 Cafe a fine place for a quiet business lunch or dinner. The menu features an assortment of soups, salads, burgers and omelets.

SCALLOP-CORN GINGER SOUP

GRILLED HOISIN CHICKEN

WILD RICE

ORANGE CREAM PUDDING

Vouvray
Petit Sirah
Serves 4

SCALLOP-CORN GINGER SOUP

4 cups fish stock
1 pound sea scallops
2 cups fresh corn cut from the cob
2 tablespoons rice wine
1 tablespoon finely chopped fresh ginger
3 tablespoons chopped scallions
1 tablespoon sugar
Salt and pepper to taste
1/2 cup heavy cream
1 tablespoon butter
3 tablespoons finely chopped fresh chives for garnish

1. In a medium-sized pot, bring the fish stock to a simmer, then add the scallops and corn. Simmer for 2 or 3 minutes. Add the rice wine, ginger, scallions, sugar, salt, and pepper. Simmer 1 minute more. Cool briefly, then purée the mixture in a blender. Return the soup to the pot and bring to a simmer. Adjust the seasonings and add the cream and butter, stirring to mix well.
2. Ladle into individual bowls or into a tureen and garnish with the chives.

GRILLED HOISIN CHICKEN

For the Marinade:
1 teaspoon fresh or 1/2 teaspoon dried thyme leaves
3 tablespoons hoisin sauce
2 tablespoons rice wine
1 tablespoon olive oil
4 (4-ounce) chicken breast halves, boned

1. Mix the marinade ingredients together and rub each chicken breast on both sides. Cover with plastic wrap and marinate for 30 minutes at room temperature or for 1 hour in the refrigerator. If refrigerated, bring to room temperature before grilling.
2. When the grill is hot or when the charcoal turns ash white, quickly grill the chicken breasts on both sides, being careful not to overcook them.

ORANGE CREAM PUDDING

2 cups orange juice
1 envelope unflavored gelatin
1/2 cup milk
1/2 cup sugar
2 eggs
1 cup heavy cream

1. Bring the orange juice to a simmer. Add the gelatin and dissolve it in the hot juice. Place the orange juice-gelatin liquid in a blender and add the milk. Blend until smooth.
2. Then add the sugar and eggs and blend for 10 seconds. Add the cream and continue to blend for another 20 seconds.
3. Spoon into individual serving dishes, cover with plastic wrap and chill for at least 3 hours before serving.

Evan Kleiman is a chef and co-proprietor of Angeli and Trattoria Angeli, Los Angeles restaurants which feature "New Italian Cooking." Viana La Place has also gained experience in the kitchens of California's restaurants. Both are accomplished chefs whose recipes represent the fashion in which Italians often take their meals: foods prepared ahead and served at room temperature.

Evan Kleiman and Viana La Place, whose latest book is *Cucina Pasta*, served this "new Italian dinner" at Mezzanotte on March 17, 1988. The recipes for the grilled bread with olive paste and salsa cruda and the swordfish are found in *Cucina Fresca*, an earlier book by Kleiman and La Place. The pasta dish is from *Cucina Pasta*.

The trend toward casual trattorias and "New Italian Cuisine" is evident at Mezzanote. Located in the city's Fairmount section, Mezzanote, which means "midnight," offers food and drink in a friendly atmosphere. Enter the bar area and enjoy a beer, Campari and soda, or a glass of wine while you watch the latest sports event on television. On the way to the dining room, which is fitted with comfortable black-topped tables and matching chairs, take a glance at the antipasto table brimming with roasted peppers, sun-dried tomatoes, fresh mozzarella, and other room temperature fare.

OLIVE PASTE

(Pesto di Olive)

GRILLED BREAD

TIMBALE OF EGGPLANT WITH TUBETTI

(Pasta 'ncasciata)

GRILLED SWORDFISH

RAW TOMATO AND BASIL SAUCE

(Salsa Cruda)

MIXED FRUIT SALAD WITH MINT AND MARASCHINO LIQUEUR

Chianti

Serves 4

OLIVE PASTE *(Pesto di Olive)*

1/2 cup oil-cured black olives, pitted
4 canned flat anchovy fillets
1 tablespoon minced fresh basil leaves, or 1 tablespoon minced fresh rosemary leaves, or 1 teaspoon dried rosemary leaves, crumbled
1 garlic clove, peeled
1 tablespoon capers
1 heaping tablespoon minced fresh fennel bulb
1 teaspoon grated orange zest
4 tablespoons olive oil
3 to 4 tablespoons lemon juice
Dash cayenne pepper

1. Combine all the ingredients in a food processor or blender. Process just until the ingredients are combined but before the mixture becomes too smooth. A little texture adds interest. For a coarser texture, finely chop the olives, anchovy fillets, garlic and capers and stir in remaining ingredients.
2. Serve a very thin coating on grilled bread.

Makes 3/4 cup. The spread lasts 1 week refrigerated.

TIMBALE OF EGGPLANT WITH TUBETTI
(Pasta 'ncasciata)

2 to 3 firm, glossy medium eggplants
Salt
Extra-virgin olive oil
1 large garlic clove, peeled and lightly crushed
1 (28-ounce) can imported Italian tomatoes, seeded and puréed
Salt and freshly ground black pepper to taste
Handful fresh basil leaves, coarsely chopped
1 pound imported tubetti
2 ounces good quality Italian salami, diced
3/4 pound fresh mozzarella, cut into small dice
1 cup freshly grated Pecorino Romano cheese, plus additional for table use
3 hard-cooked eggs, peeled and sliced

1. Slice the eggplants lengthwise, approximately 1/4-inch thick. Salt and let drain in colander for about 1 hour. Pat dry with paper towels.
2. Heat the extra-virgin olive oil to measure 1/2-inch up the side of a large frying pan. When the oil is very hot but not smoking, fry eggplant slices until golden brown on both sides. Fry 1 layer at a time without crowding the pan. Drain on paper towels. Reserve 3 tablespoons of the oil.
3. Line a large, round baking dish with the eggplant slices, overlapping them slightly. Set aside. Chop any remaining eggplant and set aside.
4. Sauté the garlic in the oil. Add the puréed tomatoes and season with salt and pepper. Cook over medium heat until the sauce thickens, about 15 minutes. Stir in the basil and set aside.
5. Cook the pasta in a generous amount of salted boiling water. Drain well. In a large bowl, combine the pasta and the tomato sauce. Toss and add the salami, mozzarella, 1 cup Pecorino Romano cheese and the chopped eggplant.
6. Layer the sliced eggs over the eggplant slices in the baking dish. Top with the pasta mixture and pack it down slightly. Bake in a preheated 400-degree oven for 20 minutes.
7. Carefully invert onto a serving platter. Blot the surface with paper towels. Cut into wedges. Serve with additional cheese on the side.

GRILLED SWORDFISH

2 pounds swordfish, cut into large, 1/2-inch-thick steaks
Olive oil
Coarse salt and freshly ground pepper to taste
1 recipe salsa cruda

1. Brush the steaks with olive oil. Grill very closely to the source of heat, about 4 to 5 minutes total cooking time, turning once. Place the fish on a serving dish and season with salt and pepper.
2. Spoon some of the salsa cruda over the fish and let cool. Do not refrigerate. Serve with extra sauce on the side.

RAW TOMATO AND BASIL SAUCE
(Salsa Cruda)

2 pounds firm ripe red tomatoes
2 garlic cloves, peeled and minced
1/4 cup finely chopped fresh basil leaves
1/2 cup fruity olive oil
Coarse salt and freshly ground pepper to taste

1. If the skins of the tomatoes are particularly tough, plunge them into boiling water for 5 seconds and peel them.
2. Core, seed and dice the tomatoes. Combine with the garlic, basil, and olive oil in a bowl. Season with salt and pepper to taste.
3. Marinate for 1 hour before using.

You can serve this sauce on any grilled fish.

Makes 3 cups

Leslie Land began her career in the kitchen during her college days at the University of California, Berkeley, where she was chosen by her roommates and friends to prepare meals and plan parties. She worked with Alice Waters at Chez Panisse, became a caterer, gave it all up and moved to Maine.

Her often amusing food columns appear in the *Philadelphia Inquirer*, the *San Francisco Examiner*, and *The New York Times*. On March 17, 1989, Land prepared this meal at the Restaurant School. All recipes are from *Reading Between the Recipes*, Land's first book.

The Restaurant School, a unique Philadelphia institution which grew out of the restaurant renaissance, is located in a fine old Walnut Street mansion, not far from Rittenhouse Square. Its high ceilings, wall mouldings, and tall windows speak of the graciousness of 19th century Philadelphia. Its regular menus rotate with the course of work of in-residence student chefs. They are prepared under the direction of Restaurant School Director Danny Liberatoscioli and faculty member Andrew Schloss. Although a training ground for chefs, the school is run as a regular restaurant.

BRAISED LEEKS WITH BERRY VINEGAR

MIXED GREEN SALAD

SEASHELL PASTA WITH CRAB, SPRING PEAS AND MUSHROOMS IN CREAM

APRICOT GINGER FLORENTINES

Fumé Blanc
Chardonnay

BRAISED LEEKS WITH BERRY VINEGAR

1 1/2 pounds leeks, white and pale chartreuse parts only
1/4 cup olive oil
1/2 teaspoon salt
2 or 3 tablespoons blackberry or raspberry vinegar (available in specialty stores)
5 or 6 fresh blackberries or raspberries as garnish, optional

1. Trim and clean the leeks and cut into 1-inch lengths. Put the olive oil in a heavy, lidded skillet big enough to hold the pieces in one layer and arrange the leeks in the pan. Sprinkle them with salt, cover, and place over very low heat. Steam-braise, shaking the pan so the leeks cook evenly, 20 to 25 minutes, or until they are very tender when tested with a knife point. Try not to let them brown.
2. Transfer the cooked leeks and their juices to a shallow serving dish, mix in 2 tablespoons of the vinegar, and allow to cool. Let marinate at room temperature for an hour or so, then taste and adjust the vinegar if necessary. These keep well, refrigerated, though the berry dye they absorb from the vinegar eventually makes them a rather strange color. Garnish with berries if desired.

SEASHELL PASTA WITH CRAB, SPRING PEAS AND MUSHROOMS IN CREAM

2 teaspoons salt
1 teaspoon olive oil
1 cup whipping cream (30% butterfat, not ultrapasteurized)
3/4 pound cooked crabmeat, picked over to remove any bits of shell
1/8 teaspoon freshly grated nutmeg
3 tablespoons butter
1 cup very fresh mushrooms, wiped but not washed, and coarsely chopped
1 pound seashell pasta
3/4 cup fresh peas, about 3/4 pound in the shell
3/4 cup lightly piled freshly grated Parmesan cheese
1/4 pound super-thinly sliced prosciutto or Westphalian ham, cut into thin slivers
Kosher salt

1. Combine the salt and oil with at least a gallon of water in a large kettle, cover, and put on to boil for the pasta.
2. Put the cream, crabmeat, and nutmeg in a small, heavy saucepan and put it somewhere warm to heat and infuse without actually cooking - the back of the stove, if you have that kind of stove.

   Warm the serving plates.
3. In a small skillet, melt the butter over medium-high heat and add the mushrooms when it foams. Saute them, stirring often, until they are well browned, then set them aside in the same place as the crabmeat cream to keep warm.
4. When the water boils, uncover the pan and slowly stir in the pasta, dribbling it a bit at a time so the water never stops boiling. Cook about 8 minutes, or until a test shell is almost but not quite done. Add the peas and cook 2 minutes more, then drain thoroughly and return to the pot.
5. Pour in the crabmeat cream and toss madly, then add everything else except the kosher salt, stirring and tossing as you add so the tidbits are well distributed. Portion the pasta onto the warm plates and pass the kosher salt for the diners to sprinkle at will.

APRICOT GINGER FLORENTINES

1/2 cup heavy cream (Do not use ultrapasteurized)
3 tablespoons sugar
1/2 cup slivered blanched almonds
4 tablespoons diced dried apricots
4 tablespoons diced candied ginger, freed of excess sugar
Pinch of salt
Approximately 1/4 cup flour
Unsalted butter and flour for the cookie sheets
4 1/2 ounces white chocolate

1. Preheat the oven to 350 degrees. Combine the cream and sugar and set aside. Chop half the almonds just enough to make pieces the size of the fruit dice and grind the remainder cornmeal fine.
2. Stir the fruit and nuts into the cream, along with the salt, then stir in half the flour. Continue adding flour by tablespoons until you have a soft dough. Butter a square of foil and make a test cookie, dropping on a tablespoon of dough and gently spreading it out as thin as possible in view of the lumps.
3. Bake 10 to 12 minutes, or until nicely brown around the edges. The cookie should be very flat and crisp. Add more flour if it ran all over; thin with milk if by some unhappy chance the dough is too thick. Butter and flour two cookie sheets, then form and bake the remaining cookies and cool on racks.
4. Chop or grate the chocolate so it melts evenly over hot, not quite simmering water. Allow to cool to warm room temperature, then use to paint the bottoms of the cookies.

Makes about 30 (3-inch) cookies

Deborah Madison's fascination with unusual fruits and vegetables and the herbs which enhance them led her to become one of the pioneers of the new vegetarianism. As the former chef at Greens Restaurant on San Francisco Bay, she developed an elegant style and a loyal following. Deborah Madison is the co-author, with Edward Espe Brown, of *The Greens Cookbook* and is currently a menu consultant, living in Arizona.

Along with Steve Poses, proprietor of The USA Cafe, Madison created an unusual vegetarian meal on March 18, 1988. All recipes are from *The Greens Cookbook*.

The USA Cafe is perched atop The Commissary, Philadelphia's first gourmet cafeteria. It's located a few blocks from Rittenhouse Square. Proprietor Steve Poses opened the cafe, complete with waiter service, one flight up from his famous cafeteria.

The USA Cafe serves New American fare, but the accents may be Mexican, Italian, Thai, or Chinese. A variety of soups and salads are offered, including Poses's unique version of the all American Cobb Salad. Pastas are made fresh and are often garnished with shrimp or scallops. Game hens, fresh fish, and prime beef also play a prominent role at the USA Cafe. Desserts such as Carrot Cake, Strawberry Tarts, or Killer Chocolate Cake end the meal.

The USA Cafe has a fine wine list with the accent on California. Beer is also available.

MENU

EARLY SPRING SOUP

OLIVE OIL BREAD

(Focaccia)

ALMOND-PINE NUT TART

Beringer Chenin Blanc
Glen Ellen Cabernet Sauvignon
Serves 4

EARLY SPRING SOUP

For the Stock:
Use water or boil 8 cups water with some leek greens, chard stems and parsley.
For the Soup:
3 tablespoons butter or olive oil
4 to 5 small leeks, white parts only (about 8 ounces), sliced
1 medium potato, scrubbed and sliced
3 to 4 celery stalks (about 1 cup), diced
Salt
1/4 pound snow peas, strings removed, roughly chopped, or 1/2 cup frozen peas
8 branches parsley or chervil
3 lovage leaves or 1 handful sorrel leaves, roughly chopped
6 cups water or light stock
Nutmeg
Lemon juice or Champagne vinegar to taste
Cream or crème fraiche, optional
Pepper, optional

1. Warm the butter or oil in a soup pot, add the leeks, potato and celery, 1 teaspoon salt and 1 cup water. Cover the pot and stew the vegetables over medium-low heat for 15 minutes. Stir once or twice to make sure the vegetables aren't sticking to the bottom of the pot; if they are, add more water.
2. Add the snow peas, or peas, herbs and greens, cover, and continue to cook until the greens have wilted, about 5 minutes. Add the 6 cups water or stock and bring to a boil; simmer for 10 minutes.
3. Let the soup cool briefly; transfer to a blender and purée. If all the strings have not been removed from the peas, the soup may be fibrous. Check to see if it is smooth and if not, pass the soup through a food mill or chinoise.
4. Season the soup to taste with a few scrapings of nutmeg and lemon juice or vinegar. Add salt if needed. Thin it with cream, if desired, or serve it with crème fraiche and freshly ground black pepper.
5. Gently reheat the soup before serving.

NOTE: Leftover soup freezes well. But do not add cream or crème fraiche before freezing.

OLIVE OIL BREAD *(Focaccia)*

1 package active dry yeast (2 1/2 teaspoons)
1 cup tepid water
1 teaspoon salt
3 tablespoons virgin olive oil
Pinch sugar
2 1/2 cups unbleached white flour or a mixture of whole wheat and white
Coarse sea salt

1. Dissolve the yeast in the warm water with the salt, olive oil and sugar. Stir in the flour in 2 or 3 additions. Once a dough has formed, turn it out onto a board dusted with flour and knead it for several minutes, adding only enough flour to keep the dough from sticking. When the dough is smooth and shiny, set it in a lightly oiled bowl, turn it over once, cover and put it in a warm place to rise until it is doubled in bulk, about 30 to 40 minutes.
2. After the dough has risen, turn it onto the counter and shape it with a rolling pin into 1 large or 2 small ovals, about 1/2-inch thick. Make several cuts in the dough in the center of the oval - parallel or fan-shaped cuts, or many little diagonal slices - then pull the edges of the dough apart, opening the cuts to give the loaf a latticed appearance. If you are going to bake the bread on a pizza stone, transfer the loaf to a well-floured peel. Otherwise, put it on an oiled baking sheet. Brush the bread with olive oil, sprinkle it lightly with coarse sea salt and set it aside to rise for 20 minutes.
3. Preheat the oven to 450 degrees. If using a pizza stone, warm it for 20 minutes.
4. After it has risen, slide the dough onto the stone, or put the baking sheet in the oven. Bake in the top third of the oven for 20 to 30 minutes, or until the bread is nicely browned. You can spray the bread and oven with a fine mist of water 2 or 3 times during the first 10 minutes of the baking to help give the bread a good crust. Serve hot from the oven, with or without butter.

ALMOND-PINE NUT TART

1 recipe Sweet Tart Dough, see page 95
1/2 cup almonds
1/3 cup sugar
Pinch salt
2 eggs
1 teaspoon vanilla
A few drops almond extract
1/2 cup unsalted butter, room temperature
2 tablespoons flour
1/2 teaspoon baking powder
3 to 4 tablespoons raspberry or apricot jam
1/2 cup pine nuts
Powdered sugar

1. Prepare the sweet tart dough and line a 9-inch tart pan with removable bottom. Partially bake it according to directions given in the recipe.
2. Bring a small pan of water to a boil, add the almonds, turn off the heat and let them sit for 1 minute. Drain them, then slip off the skins and rub them in a clean kitchen towel to dry.
3. Grind the almonds in a food processor fitted with a metal blade for about 45 seconds. Add the sugar, salt, eggs, vanilla, and almond extract. Process another 10 seconds. Add the butter, flour, and baking powder and process long enough to make a smooth batter, about 10 seconds.
4. Preheat the oven to 375 degrees. Spread a thick layer of jam over the tart shell; cover it with the almond filling. Set the pine nuts over the top and bake the tart until the surface is firm and browned, about 30 minutes. Remove it from the oven and let it cool. Dust it with powdered sugar. Serve by itself or with soft mounds of sweetened whipped cream.

Makes 1 (9-inch) tart

SWEET TART DOUGH

1 cup all-purpose flour
Pinch salt
1 tablespoon sugar
1/4 teaspoon grated orange peel
4 ounces unsalted butter, room temperature
1 tablespoon water
1/2 teaspoon vanilla

To make dough by hand:

1. Combine the flour, salt, sugar, and orange peel in a bowl. Cut the butter into small pieces, add it to the dry ingredients and rub the mixture between your fingers to make a coarse meal. A pastry cutter or two knives can also be used.
2. Combine the water and the vanilla, stir them into the flour-butter mixture with a fork and then mix lightly with your fingers until the pastry comes together when pressed.
3. Gather the dough into a ball, press it into a round disk, wrap it in plastic and let it rest for 1/2 hour. If it is a warm day and the butter is very soft, let it rest in the refrigerator.

To make dough in a food processor:

1. Combine the flour, salt, sugar, and orange peel. Then add the butter, cut into small pieces and process until a coarse meal has formed, 10 to 15 seconds, depending on how soft the butter is.
2. Combine the water and vanilla and pour it into the flour-butter mixture while the machine is running and process for just 5 seconds. Do not let the dough form a ball. Instead, empty the contents of the bowl onto your work surface, gather them together with your hands and press the dough into a ball. Flatten it into a disk, wrap it in plastic, and set it aside for 1/2 hour in the refrigerator, or freeze the dough for future use.
3. Because the dough is soft and buttery, use your hands to line the pan, rather than attempt to roll it out. Generally it seems to work best to shape the sides first, then the bottom. Press the dough into the pan, forming sides of even thickness that rise about 1/4 inch above the rim.
4. Using the heel of your hand, press the dough evenly over the bottom. Make it somewhat thinner closest to the rim because the sides will inevitably slump a little during the baking, filling in that area between the rim and the bottom. After the bottom is shaped, go back to the sides and reshape any sections that need it.

5. Cover the shell lightly with foil and put it in the freezer for at least 1/2 hour, or until the dough is firmly set in place. At this point the tart shell can be baked or wrapped well and frozen for future use. Freezing the dough makes it unnecessary to line it with foil and pie weights while baking.
6. To bake the shell, preheat the oven to 400 degrees. Place the shell in the lower third of the oven. Check it after 5 minutes; use the point of a sharp knife to pierce any large air bubbles that may have formed. If the shell is going to be filled and baked further, cook it until it is lightly browned, about 10 to 12 minutes. If it is not going to be baked again, bake a few minutes longer until it is well browned all over, at least 15 minutes in all.

Makes 1 (9-inch) tart

Film producer Ismail Merchant cooks fine Indian cuisine wherever his travels take him. If a movie is being filmed in England, Merchant takes up the fry pan and prepares the dishes which make him feel at home.

He is the author of *Ismail Merchant's Indian Cuisine*, and his delightful film, *A Room with a View*, is an Academy Award winner. Along with chef/proprietor Bill Hoffman, Merchant created this Indian dinner at Carolina's on March 26, 1987.

Carolina's has been described as "grandma's dining room," not just because of its cozy, casual ambience, but also due to the American fare served up by chef/owner Bill Hoffman.

Located near Rittenhouse Square, Carolina's dining room features a tin ceiling and bentwood cane chairs covered with green fabric that matches the curtains. Paintings by Philadelphia artist Marc Whitney, who specializes in neighborhood scenes, are set off by the soft, cream walls.

The menu is an unusual mix of international and American regional dishes. On any given day, Hoffman presents three different pastas; Thai-French entrees; a selection of fish, including salmon and local bluefish; and Mexican favorites. Yet Carolina's is noted for its Maryland Crabcakes, Sautéed Liver with Shallots, Pork Chops, and Veal Loaf with real mashed potatoes just like grandma used to make.

The bar area is popular with the locals and people who work in center city. It features a large array of domestic and imported beer, along with a selection of wine by the glass. The wine specials change two or three times a week and include vintages from California, Australia, France, Italy, and Portugal.

POTATO WATERCRESS SOUP

(Aloo aur Hari Pati ka Shorba)

SHRIMP WITH MUSTARD AND DILL

(Rai-Walla Jhingha)

INDIAN RICE PUDDING

(Kheer)

Babcock Johannisberg Riesling 1985
Zind Humbrecht Gewürztraminer (Alsace) 1984

Serves 6

POTATO WATERCRESS SOUP
(Aloo aur Hari Pati ka Shorba)

4 large potatoes
4 tablespoons butter
2 medium-size onions, peeled and chopped
3 3/4 cups chicken stock
4 large garlic cloves, peeled and chopped
1 1/2 teaspoons freshly ground white pepper
1 bunch watercress, stems removed
Salt to taste
2 1/2 cups milk

1. Cover the potatoes with water in a saucepan and boil about 15 to 20 minutes until very tender, with the skins on or off, as you prefer. (The skins are healthy and good and the soup will look agreeably speckled if you leave them on.) Drain the potatoes.
2. Melt the butter in a large saucepan over low heat, add the onions and cook until they are soft but do not color, about 8 to 10 minutes. Remove from heat.
3. Add the chicken stock to the onions, add the garlic, potatoes and pepper. Bring to a simmer and cook for 25 minutes. Sprinkle the watercress on top of the simmering liquid without mixing in and continue cooking for another 5 minutes.
4. Purée the mixture in a food processor or blender, in stages if necessary. Season with salt. Return to the saucepan.
5. Add milk and heat the soup until it is very hot but does not boil.

NOTE: To serve soup cold, simply stir the milk into the puréed mixture, cool and chill. Serve the soup garnished with fresh watercress leaves or with about 3 peeled, thinly sliced garlic cloves scattered over the top. Any leftover soup will keep in the refrigerator for about 2 days.

SHRIMP WITH MUSTARD AND DILL
(Rai-Walla Jhingha)

1 cup Dijon mustard
2 teaspoons cayenne pepper
2 garlic cloves, finely chopped
1 teaspoon caraway seeds
1/4 teaspoon tumeric
Salt to taste
2 pounds raw shrimp, shelled, cleaned, washed and dried
1/4 cup vegetable oil
1 large bunch fresh dill, finely chopped

1. Combine the mustard, cayenne pepper, garlic, caraway seeds, tumeric, and salt to taste. Add the shrimp and blend well. Cover and refrigerate for at least 1 hour and up to 6 hours.
2. Heat the oil in a deep frying pan over medium heat. When hot, add the shrimp, shaking them to remove most of the marinade. Stir well, cover and cook for 3 to 4 minutes, or until they just become firm.
3. Sprinkle dill over shrimp and stir well. Serve immediately with boiled rice and the remaining marinade as a sauce.

INDIAN RICE PUDDING *(Kheer)*

1/2 cup long-grain rice
3 1/4 cups water
5 3/4 cups milk
1 cup sugar
1/4 cup dried milk
1 tablespoon rose water
6 to 8 blanched almonds, chopped
10 to 12 shelled, unsalted pistachios, chopped
1/4 cup seedless raisins

1. Boil the rice in water until the rice is very soft.
2. Heat the milk and sugar in another saucepan and bring to a boil.
3. Immediately reduce the heat and stir in the softened rice. Continue cooking over medium-low heat, stirring, until the mixture becomes thick.
4. Add the dried milk and stir in well.
5. Add the rose water, almonds, pistachios, and raisins. Remove from heat.
6. Let the pudding cool and serve at room temperature.

Carlo Middione & Ecco

Carlo Middione is a second-generation Sicilian-American who was the Italian specialist on the faculty of the California Culinary Academy for Chefs. He is chef-owner of Vivande, the Italian restaurant/delicatessen in San Francisco.

Middione, whose zest for Italian fare is evident in his warm, friendly manner, is the author of *Pasta: Cooking it, Loving it* and the award-winning *The Food of Southern Italy*.

Middione and chef-proprietor Beatrice Nichols presented this meal at Ecco on March 17 and 18, 1989. All recipes are from *The Food of Southern Italy*.

The French say "voilà," the Italians say, "ecco." Roughly translated, the word which chef/proprietor Beatrice Nichols used to name her restaurant means "here it is." The intimate, one-dining room restaurant has an air of soft, casual elegance. The room is surrounded by windows and features an open kitchen, blue-green walls, charcoal gray banquettes, and a hand-painted abstract watercolor mural.

The cuisine is eclectic with special emphasis on Northern Italian dishes. Patrons watch Executive Chef Michael McNally turn out noted dishes such as Boneless Breast of Duck with Passion Fruit Sauce, accompanied by Spinach Strudel; Grilled Tuna or Swordfish with Chilled Relish or Tapenade; California-style Buckwheat Crepes served with three types of salmon, grilled, tartar, and smoked. Fresh pasta plays an important part in the cuisine at Ecco. Ricotta and Roasted Garlic Ravioli with Rosemary Oil or Penne in Light Saffron Cream with Asparagus and Pancetta are among the offerings. Desserts, which are made on the premises, always include something chocolate; fresh fruit, ice cream, and mousse-of-the-day round out the list.

The wine list emphasizes California wines from the Napa and Sonoma Valleys, as well as fine Australian selections.

MENU

PENNE WITH ASPARAGUS

(Penne con gli Asparagi)

LAMB CHOPS CALABRIAN STYLE

(Costolettine di Agnello alla Calabrese)

WALNUT CAKE

(Torta di Noci)

Aglianico del Vulture or Etna Rosso
Montepulciano d'Abruzzo

Serves 4

Penne with Asparagus
(Penne con gli Asparagi)

1 pound thin, tender and fresh asparagus, well washed, trimmed and cut into 2-inch pieces
1/4 cup virgin olive oil
2 large garlic cloves, peeled and well crushed
1 1/2 pounds tomatoes, cored, peeled and well crushed
14 ounces penne
1 cup grated pecorino cheese, plus more for the table
2 large eggs
Salt and freshly ground black pepper to taste

1. Cook the asparagus in boiling salted water for 4 minutes. Drain and reserve for later.
2. Heat the olive oil in a large frying pan over a medium flame, add the garlic and fry it until it is deep gold. Add the tomatoes and stir well. Cook the sauce for about 10 minutes and keep it hot but not simmering.
3. Meanwhile, boil plenty of water in a large pot and add salt. Cook the penne really al dente. You should be able to actually chew them. When the penne are done, drain them, leaving in just a bit of the cooking water.
4. Mix together in a large, heated casserole dish the penne and the asparagus. Add the cup of cheese and mix everything again. Break the eggs into a small dish, beat them lightly, add them to the penne and the asparagus and mix once more.
5. (Adding the cheese before the eggs creates a kind of insulation to keep the eggs from becoming too hot and accidentally curdling.) When you have a nice, glossy, well-coated mass of penne, asparagus, cheese, and eggs, add the tomato sauce and stir everything until it is well blended. Add salt and pepper to taste.
6. Serve the penne on heated plates immediately. Pass a bit more grated pecorino cheese at the table.

LAMB CHOPS CALABRIAN STYLE
(Costolettine di Agnello alla Calabrese)

2 large red bell peppers (use green if red not available)
1 large garlic clove, minced
About 1/2 cup virgin olive oil, divided
2 large juicy lemons
8 baby artichokes, washed and trimmed
1 teaspoon salt and to taste
Freshly ground black pepper to taste
1/2 pound mushrooms
8 rib lamb chops with long bone left in
2 tablespoons capers
8 anchovy filets

1. Wash the bell peppers and dry them. Put them on the burner plate over a high gas flame and let the flames lick up around them. After one side has become charred and very black, turn the pepper around with tongs and burn the skin on the other side. When they are totally black, set them aside to cool on a dish.

   If you have an electric stove, char the peppers in a very hot broiler and follow the directions as for gas stove.

2. When the peppers are cool enough to handle, lay them down on a board or on the edge of your sink and scrape the blackened skin off of them. (It should slip right off.) Cut the peppers open, scrape out and discard the seeds and remove and discard the core. Cut the peppers into slices about 1/4-inch thick and put them on a plate. Scatter the garlic all over them, drizzle on about 2 tablespoons of virgin olive oil, and squeeze on the juice of 1/4 of a lemon. Set the peppers aside for later use.

3. Soak the baby artichokes in cold water to clean them and in another large bowl prepare 3 quarts of acidulated water by adding 3 tablespoons of lemon juice. Peel off the outer tough leaves of the artichokes until the inner, yellow leaves appear, dipping the artichoke you are working on in the acidulated water occasionally to keep it from turning black. Leave each soaking in the acidulated water. When you have finished this part of the job, remove each one from the water, and, with a sharp paring knife, trim the bottom so that it looks clean and neat. The bottom is edible and choice, so don't take off any more than is necessary. Cut about 25 percent of the top off, and cut each artichoke into quarters lengthwise.

4. Place the artichokes in a small saucepan, cover them with cold water and add 3 slices of lemon, skin and all, 1 teaspoon of salt, 4 grindings of fresh black pepper and 2 tablespoons of olive oil. Turn the heat to medium, bring the artichokes to a simmer

and cook them for 10 minutes, or until they are tender. The liquid should be evaporated, except for the oil, which should remain to coat them. If the artichokes are done and there is too much liquid, quickly remove them from the water with a slotted spoon and put them temporarily into a dish. Reduce the liquid over high heat until only the oil remains. Remove the lemon slices and discard them. Put the artichokes back into the oil and stir them. Set them aside for later use.

5. Wipe the mushrooms clean with a paper or kitchen towel. If they are large, cut them into quarters. In a frying pan that will just hold the mushrooms, heat 2 tablespoons of olive oil over high heat, add the mushrooms and stir them. Sauté them for 5 minutes or until they become golden. Do not overcook them. Squeeze on the juice of 1/2 lemon and with the heat still high, swirl and stir everything around to evaporate the lemon juice. If there is any liquid left, remove the mushrooms from the frying pan with a slotted spoon, put them onto a bowl or dish to cool and reduce the pan juice over high heat until it is thick and there is very little of it. Pour this remaining juice on the mushrooms. Set them aside until later.

6. Gently pound the meat with a meat bat to less than 1/4-inch thickness. Add salt and pepper to taste. Heat 1 tablespoon olive oil in a large frying pan to almost smoking, quickly fry the chops for about 1 minute each on each side and put them aside on a heated plate. They should be well browned outside but pink inside, not raw or even blood rare, just pink.

7. Assemble the chops attractively on a serving platter. They are very pretty if you place the bones pointing toward the middle of the platter or toward the outside of the platter. In between the bones, where there is plenty of space, carefully put the bell peppers, artichoke pieces, and mushrooms in little heaps. Scatter a few capers on top of these vegetables, and then, either on top of the vegetables or off to the side, place the anchovies. (The vegetables do not need to be hot, but the meat does. The vegetables are more like garnishes in this dish, as opposed to a regular portion.)

NOTE: Ask your butcher to cut the lamb rib bones so that they are about 6 inches long. Take the chine bone (the chine is the part of the back bone to which the ribs are attached and is usually left on chop cuts) off the ribs using a heavy cleaver, or carefully dissect it off, or have the butcher do it. (Leave the rib bone on. It looks nice and makes it easy to pick the meat up with the fingers.)

WALNUT CAKE *(Torta di Noci)*

4 ounces (8 tablespoons or 1/2 cup) sweet butter at room temperature, plus butter for cake pan
2/3 cup granulated sugar
1 large egg
2 tablespoons Jamaican dark rum
Zest of 1 lemon
1 teaspoon vanilla extract
1 1/2 teaspoons baking powder
2 1/4 cups finely grated shelled walnuts, resembling meal
1 cup all-purpose flour plus flour for dusting cake pan
Confectioner's sugar

1. Preheat the oven to 350 degrees. Grease a 9-inch cake pan with butter and sprinkle flour all over it, shaking the pan well to get a thin, even coating. Bang the pan once to dislodge excess flour, and discard flour.
2. Cream the butter with the sugar in an electric mixer with the whisk attachment. When the butter and sugar are well creamed and very soft and smooth, add the egg, rum, lemon zest, vanilla, and the baking powder, and mix well. Add the walnuts, a little at a time, and keep mixing. When all the walnuts are in, add the flour, a bit at a time, from a sifter or sieve. This will keep it from lumping. The batter should be rather dense.
3. Pour the batter into the prepared cake pan, spreading it evenly with a spatula to make the top level, and place the cake in the top part of the oven to bake for about 1 hour, or until it is firm to the touch.
4. Take it out of the oven and carefully turn it out of the pan to cool on a cooling rack. The torta di noci is actually better the next day. When it is cool, wrap it in plastic wrap, but do not refrigerate it. Wrapped thus, it will keep for about 4 days. Just before serving it, sprinkle confectioner's sugar all over the top.

Makes 1 (9-inch) cake

Known throughout the world as an author, teacher and food consultant, Jacques Pepin was chef to three French Presidents and presided over the kitchens at the Plaza Atheneé in Paris and Le Pavillon in New York. Born in Bourg-en-Bresse, France, Jacques Pepin came to the United States in 1959. He is the author of *A French Chef Cooks at Home*, *The Art of Cooking*, and *Everyday Cooking with Jacques Pepin*, the companion guide to his Public Television series.

Pepin prepared this dinner with Executive Chef John Jividen of Ridgewell's at Pier 19, overlooking the Delaware River, beneath the lights of the Benjamin Franklin Bridge, on March 18, 1989. All recipes are from *The Art of Cooking*.

"ANGRY" TROUT IN HOT PECAN SAUCE

CHICKEN BREASTS STUFFED WITH CHERVIL MOUSSE AND VEGETABLE STUFFED PEPPERS

BLACK AND RED CURRANT CAKE

Chaddsford Chardonnay

Serves 4

"ANGRY" TROUT IN HOT PECAN SAUCE

4 (8-ounce) trout, gutted
1/4 teaspoon salt
1/3 cup flour
2 tablespoons butter
2 tablespoons corn oil
For the Hot Pecan Sauce:
1/2 cup pecan pieces
1 tablespoon butter
1/2 teaspoon chopped serrano or jalapeño pepper (optional)
1/4 teaspoon anise seed
3/4 cup diced mushrooms (or trimmings from mushroom garnish)
1/3 cup chicken stock
2 tablespoons lemon juice
1/4 teaspoon salt
1/4 teaspoon freshly ground black pepper
2 tablespoons butter (final addition)
For the Garnish:
Parsley
4 large mushrooms, the cap for decoration and the remainder - about 3/4 cup trimmings - diced for use in the sauce
1 tablespoon lemon juice
For the Hush Puppies:
1 cup flour
1/2 cup cornmeal
1 tablespoon baking powder
1/4 teaspoon freshly ground black pepper
1/4 teaspoon salt
1/4 cup chopped scallions
1/4 teaspoon serrano or jalapeño pepper
1 tablespoon melted butter
2 eggs
1/2 cup milk
5 cups corn oil for frying

1. For the hush puppies, combine the dry ingredients (1 cup flour, 1/2 cup cornmeal, 1 tablespoon baking powder, 1/4 teaspoon each salt and pepper), 1/4 cup chopped scallions, 1/4 teaspoon serrano or jalapeño pepper and 1 tablespoon melted butter. Mix in the 2 eggs and 1/2 cup milk, whisking to combine well.
2. Heat about 5 cups oil (2 inches deep) to 350 degrees in a saucepan. Drop approximately 1 tablespoon of the hush puppy

dough at a time into the oil. The dough balls don't have to be completely round; if there are bits of dough sticking out here and there, the hush puppies will be crunchier.

3. Cook 5 to 6 minutes, turning the hush puppies occasionally so they brown evenly all around. Remove to paper towels to absorb the excess oil and set aside, keeping them warm.
4. For cooking the fish, lay each fish skin side down and open to lay flat. Fold the trout inward and pull the tail through the mouth. Sprinkle the fish with 1/4 teaspoon salt and dip lightly in 1/3 cup flour.
5. Heat 2 tablespoons each butter and oil in 1 very large skillet or 2 smaller ones. When hot, add the trout in 1 layer and cook over medium heat for 5 minutes. Turn and cook on the other side for 3 to 4 minutes.
6. Meanwhile, make the sauce: In a separate pan sauté 1/2 cup pecans in 1 tablespoon butter until golden. Add 1/2 teaspoon chopped hot pepper, 1/4 teaspoon anise seed and 3/4 cup diced mushrooms and sauté another minute. Add 1/3 cup chicken stock, 2 tablespoons lemon juice, 1/4 teaspoon each salt and pepper and heat to boiling. Set aside.
7. Remove the trout and place on 4 individual serving plates. Melt 2 tablespoons of butter in another skillet. When foaming and brown, combine with the pecan sauce and spoon onto the trout. Garnish with a little parsley and the optional mushroom cap. Serve immediately with the hush puppies.

CHICKEN BREASTS STUFFED WITH CHERVIL MOUSSE AND VEGETABLE STUFFED PEPPERS

4 whole boneless chicken breasts (from 2 1/2-pound chickens), cut in half

For the Mousse:

1 1/2 pounds of chicken leg meat
1/3 cup chopped ice
1 cup chervil, loose
1 cup heavy cream
1 teaspoon salt
1/4 teaspoon freshly ground black pepper

For the Vegetable-Stuffed Peppers:

8 green and red poblano peppers (or bell peppers), about 3 ounces each

For the Stuffing:

1 tablespoon butter
1 tablespoon corn oil
1 cup (1/4-inch) diced onions
1 cup (1/4-inch) diced carrots
1 cup water
2 cups cauliflower florets (cut into 1/2 to 1-inch pieces)
1 cup (1/2-inch) diced zucchini
1/2 teaspoon finely chopped garlic
1/4 teaspoon freshly ground black pepper
1/4 teaspoon salt
2 tablespoons olive oil

For Sautéeing the Chicken Breasts:

1/4 teaspoon salt
2 tablespoons butter

For the Cognac Sauce:

1 cup strong chicken stock
1/2 cup dry white wine
1 cup heavy cream
1 teaspoon potato starch dissolved in 1 tablespoon water
1 tablespoon cognac
1/4 teaspoon freshly ground black pepper
1/4 teaspoon salt

Garnish:

1 red pepper, peeled with a vegetable peeler, cut into at least 12 small rounds

1. To make the mousse, place the 1 1/2 pounds of chicken leg meat and the 1/3 cup ice in a large food processor with the 1 cup chervil. Process for about 10 seconds, clean the bowl all around with a rubber spatula, pushing the scrapings back into the mixture in the bottom of the bowl. Process 10 seconds more, clean the sides of the bowl again and process another 10 seconds.
2. Add the 1 cup cream in a slow stream along with 1 teaspoon salt and 1/4 teaspoon pepper while the machine is running and process briefly to mix. Transfer to a bowl. Notice the texture is smooth and slightly spongy. Refrigerate until ready to use.
3. Place the chicken breasts skin side up on the work surface, pull back the skin and spoon about 1/8 cup of the mousse on top of each breast. Arrange 1 of the pieces of fillet meat on 1 side of each of the breasts, pressing it into the mousse.
4. Bring the skin back on top of the mousse so it encases the whole surface. Hold a stuffed breast skin side down in the palm of one hand and try to bring the edges of the skin around to the underside of the breasts. The skin will not wrap all around. Repeat with each breast. Refrigerate, skin side down, covered, until serving time.
5. To make the peppers, arrange 8 peppers on a broiler pan and place them under a hot broiler, no more than 1 inch from the heat source, turning until the peppers blister all around, from 13 to 15 minutes. Immediately place the peppers in a plastic bag. Close the bag and set aside for 10 minutes. Steaming in their own heat in the plastic bag will help the peppers release their skin.
6. Remove the peppers from the bag and peel off the skin; it will come off fairly easily. Tear the peppers open carefully, scoop out the seeds and scrape off the membranes on the inside. Try, if possible, to leave the stem of the pepper in place as it looks more attractive this way for serving.
7. To make the stuffing, heat 1 tablespoon each butter and corn oil in a skillet. When hot, add 1 cup each diced onions and carrots. Sauté approximately 1 minute and add 1 cup of water. Cover, bring to a boil, and cook 3 minutes. Add 2 cups cauliflower and 1 cup zucchini, cover, and continue cooking for another 3 minutes, until most of the water has evaporated. Remove the lid, add 1/2 teaspoon chopped garlic, 1/4 teaspoon each pepper and salt and continue cooking until most of the water has evaporated and the mixture is sizzling. Cool to lukewarm.
8. Stuff each of the peppers with approximately 2 to 3 tablespoons of the stuffing, exercise as much care as possible, but don't worry if the peppers split a little. Fold the peppers back on top of the stuffing to reconstruct them and place in a gratin dish or casserole. Sprinkle with 2 tablespoons olive oil, cover with a piece of parchment paper and place in a 400-degree oven for 15 minutes.

9. Meanwhile, sauté the chicken breasts. Sprinkle the chicken with 1/4 teaspoon salt and heat 1 tablespoon butter each in 2 skillets, preferably non-stick. When hot, add the chicken skin side down and sauté for about 4 minutes over high heat. Cover, reduce the heat and cook gently for 10 minutes. Note that the chicken is cooked only skin side down so the meat doesn't toughen. Remove the cover from the chicken and continue cooking until the juices are reduced and the chicken is sizzling again in the fat. The chicken should be nicely browned. Remove to a platter.
10. Remove the peppers from the oven, brush them with the oil from the cooking dish, arrange in a serving dish and set aside until the chicken is ready to serve.
11. In the pan in which the chicken was cooked there will be a lot of fat in the drippings because of the skin. Boil down the drippings until the juice of the chicken crystallizes on the bottom of the skillet and creates a solidified glaze, and the fat breaks down and is clear on top. Let it sit for 1 to 2 minutes and then pour off and discard most of the fat.
12. Add 1/3 cup of water to the remaining juice, bring it to a boil and strain through a sieve. Reduce again until you have about 3 tablespoons of concentrated juice.
13. To make the sauce, bring the 1 cup chicken stock and 1/2 cup white wine to a boil and reduce to 1 cup. Add 1 cup cream, bring to the boil again and add 1 teaspoon potato starch dissolved in 1 tablespoon water. Add 1 tablespoon cognac and 1/4 teaspoon each salt and pepper and strain through a fine sieve.
14. To make pepper garnish, with a vegetable peeler, remove the skin from as much of the pepper as possible. Cut the pepper into pieces and remove the seeds. Using the 1/2-inch tip of a pastry bag tube, cut out circles, splitting them in half crosswise if too thick.
15. Arrange the chicken breasts on a serving platter, pour the sauce over them and sprinkle glacé of chicken (the concentrated juice left in the pan) on each.
16. Garnish with the red pepper rounds for color and serve with the stuffed peppers.

BLACK AND RED CURRANT CAKE

For the Sponge Cake Batter:
3 eggs, separated
3/4 cup sugar
1 teaspoon vanilla
1/4 cup corn or safflower oil
1/2 cup cake flour
1/2 cup all-purpose flour
1 teaspoon baking powder
1/2 cup milk, divided
For the Currant Filling:
1 1/2 pounds fresh red currants (about 2 cups strained)
4 egg yolks
1/2 cup sugar
1/4 cup cold water
2 envelopes gelatin (about 1 1/2 tablespoons)
4 tablespoons water
3 egg whites
2 tablespoons sugar
To Finish the Cake:
2 tablespoons raspberry brandy
1/3 cup black currant preserves, preferably with pieces of the fruit
1/4 cup currants for top of cake
1/4 cup currant jelly, melted
For Decoration:
1 cup heavy cream
1 tablespoon sugar
1/4 cup fresh currants with stems attached

1. To make cake batter, mix the 3 egg yolks, 3/4 cup sugar, and 1 teaspoon vanilla together with a whisk in a mixing bowl. Add the 1/4 cup oil, and mix just enough to incorporate. Mix the 1/2 cup each cake and all-purpose flour and 1 teaspoon baking powder together, then add to the bowl along with 1/4 cup of the milk, mixing well with the whisk. Add the remaining 1/4 cup milk and beat with the whisk for 20 to 30 seconds until the mixture is smooth and light.
2. Beat the 3 egg whites with a whisk or an electric beater until stiff but not dry. Mix 1/3 of the whites into the batter with the whisk to lighten the mixture and, using a spatula, fold in the remainder of the whites until well-incorporated.
3. Butter and flour a 10-inch springform cake pan about 2 inches high and pour the batter into it. Place on a cookie sheet and bake in a preheated 325-degree oven for 40 to 45 minutes. Let

the cake cool for 20 to 25 minutes and then unmold it onto a wire rack. Let cool further while making the filling.

4. Strain the currants through a food mill fitted with the smallest screen. If there are still seeds in the purée, strain it again through a sieve.
5. Place the 4 egg yolks in a mixer fitted with a whisk beater. Put the 1/2 cup sugar with the 1/4 cup cold water in a saucepan and stir just enough to dissolve the sugar. Place on the stove, bring to a boil and cook for about 4 to 5 minutes, until the mixture will spin a thread (about 230 degrees on a candy thermometer). Pour the hot syrup into the yolks slowly while beating at low speed. Increase the speed and continue beating on medium to high speed for about 10 minutes.
6. The mixture should be thick and creamy. Meanwhile, combine the 2 envelopes of gelatin with the 4 tablespoons of cold water and let set until the gelatin absorbs the water. Melt the softened gelatin over low heat and, when the gelatin is well melted, add it to the 2 cups of red currant purée, mixing well with a whisk. Now combine that currant-gelatin purée with the egg yolk-sugar mixture, mixing it with a whisk.
7. Beat the 3 egg whites until stiff, add the 2 tablespoons of sugar and beat again for about 30 seconds to incorporate the sugar into the whites. Spoon about 1/4 to 1/3 of the egg whites into the red currant mixture and mix with a whisk. Using a rubber spatula, gently fold the rest of the egg whites into the red currant purée.
8. When the cake is cool, trim it all around with a knife or scissors to make it approximately 9 inches in diameter. Cut cake in half to make 2 layers.
9. Sprinkle 1 layer of the cake with 1 tablespoon of the raspberry brandy and spread the 1/3 cup black currant preserves on top.
10. Line the bottom and sides of the springform pan used for baking the cake with parchment paper, oiling the paper on one side and placing the oiled side against the pan so the paper adheres well. Place the cake layer with the preserves on the bottom in the center of the pan. There should be about 1/2 inch of space all around between the cake and the pan. Spread about 1/2 of the currant filling on top and around the sides.
11. Place the other cake layer on top of the filling and push down on it gently to embed it in the filling. Sprinkle the cake with the remaining tablespoon of raspberry brandy and spread the remaining currant filling on top.
12. Sprinkle the 1/4 cup of currants on top of the cake and refrigerate for at least 1 to 2 hours until the filling is set.
13. Melt the 1/4 cup currant jelly slowly over low heat, mixing it only occasionally. When it is liquid, place over ice cold water and stir until it begins to thicken. Pour it on top of the cake and spread it all around. Place the cake back in the refrigerator for at least 2 hours.

14. At this point, remove the springform sides, then slide the cake onto a serving plate.
15. Remove the parchment paper from around the cake. It can be left on underneath.
16. Whip the 1 cup heavy cream and 1 tablespoon sugar until the cream is firm and place it in a pastry bag fitted with a star tip. Decorate the outside of the cake with the cream and arrange the 1/4 cup fresh currants, still attached to their stems, around the outside of the platter.
17. To serve, cut wedges of the cake and place on individual plates. Decorate with some of the fresh currants and a little dab of whipped cream and serve immediately.

Makes 1 (9-inch) cake

Margaret and Franco Romagnoli cook, write and appear on television together. They are the proprietors of The Romagnolis' Table, near Faneuil Hall in Boston and the stars of the successful Public Television program of the same name. They also are the authors of several books including *The Romagnolis' Table* and *Carnevale Italiano - The Romagnolis' Meatless Cookbook*.

This classically Italian Sunday dinner was created with Chef Gino Sena of La Famiglia on March 23, 1986. All recipes are from *The New Italian Cooking*.

Located in Society Hill, and owned by the Sena family, La Famiglia was created from an old, two-story warehouse. It has a cozy bar downstairs. Intimate tables covered in white linen with fresh flowers and silver candlesticks add to the soft, romantic atmosphere. Although the restaurant is famous for its fresh pasta (which Mama Sena makes every Monday) and veal, the Fried Calamari with Lemon Wedges and Diavola Sauce, Mussels Napoletana, and Salad of Arugula and Radicchio in a Light Vinaigrette are a fine way to start the meal. Five different veal dishes are featured including Grilled Chop with Porcini Mushrooms, and Medallions Sautéed in White Wine, Onion, and Rosemary.

Sweets on the dessert cart change with the seasons, but classic profiteroles with chocolate sauce, fresh fruit tarts, and chestnut cake are always available to accompany rich espresso. And Italian wines reign supreme. The selection is extraordinary.

MENU

RICE WITH LOBSTER

(Risotto all'Aragosta)

FILLET OF BEEF MARCO POLO

(Filetto alla Marco Polo)

PEPPERS WITH ONIONS AND TOMATOES

(Peperonata)

PARADISE CAKE

(Torta Paradiso)

Gavi Principessa
Pio Cesare Barolo, 1978
Moscato D'Asti

Serves 6

RICE WITH LOBSTER *(Risotto all'Aragosta)*

1 (1 1/4 to 1 1/2-pound) lobster
4 tablespoons unsalted butter
1 celery stalk, minced
1 onion, peeled and minced
1 garlic clove, peeled and minced
1 1/2 cups extra-long-grain rice
1 packet Italian powdered saffron
1/2 teaspoon salt
5 tablespoons dry sherry
3 cups hot chicken broth
2 to 3 tablespoons chopped Italian parsley

1. Bring 6 quarts water to a boil. Add 6 tablespoons salt. Place lobster in boiling water and cook for 10 minutes. Let lobster cool.
2. Remove meat from shell. Slice the tail and set aside.
3. Melt butter in a saucepan. Add minced flavorings and sauté on medium heat until limp, about 3 to 5 minutes. Add the rice, saffron, and salt. Continue cooking until rice crackles. Add sherry and cook until it has evaporated.
4. Add the hot broth and cut-up lobster claws. Cover the pan, bring to a boil, lower heat and cook for 25 minutes.
5. When rice is tender, place mixture in serving dish and dress with reserved lobster tail pieces. Top with parsley and serve immediately.

FILLET OF BEEF MARCO POLO
(Filetto alla Marco Polo)

4 1/2 pounds boneless beef tenderloin
4 slices fresh ginger
3 ounces cognac
1 small clove garlic, cut lengthwise in slivers
Dash of soy sauce
Dry red wine
Olive oil

1. Cut off and discard all long tendons and fat around the outside of the tenderloin. Place meat in a dish just large enough to accommodate it. Add ginger, cognac, garlic, and soy sauce. Pour on enough red wine to come about halfway up the side of the meat. Cover and marinate for 2 to 3 hours, turning from time to time.
2. Preheat the oven to 500 degrees. Barely cover the bottom of a sauté pan with olive oil. Heat the skillet on high heat and brown the tenderloin on all sides.
3. Transfer the meat and its juices to a roasting pan and roast for 25 minutes. Turn off the heat and allow the roast to cool in the oven until a thermometer registers 140 degrees. Slice and serve the meat on a pool of sauce.

PEPPERS WITH ONIONS AND TOMATOES
(Peperonata)

3 tablespoons olive oil
1 garlic clove
4 or 5 sweet peppers (red, green, and yellow)
3 medium onions, peeled
2 cups peeled plum tomatoes
1 teaspoon salt
Freshly ground black pepper to taste
1/3 cup dry white wine, or 3 tablespoons white wine vinegar and 3 tablespoons water

1. Put the olive oil in a good-sized pot (with a cover) over medium heat. Cut the garlic in half, add it to the oil, sauté it to a golden brown, and then discard it.
2. Cut the peppers open, discard their cores and stems, and slice them into long, thin strips. Cut the onions into quarters and cut off the bit of core at the bottom of each quarter. Add the peppers and onions to the flavored olive oil, and cook briskly, stirring constantly. As soon as they start to wilt, add the tomatoes, salt, and a few grinds of pepper. Stir well, and when the mixture is back to a boil, reduce heat, and cover the pot. Simmer for 15 to 20 minutes, stirring occasionally.
3. Raise the heat, add the wine (or wine vinegar and water), stir, and boil uncovered 5 minutes, or until the sauce has condensed a bit and the vegetables have cooked.

NOTE: This may be served either hot or cold

PARADISE CAKE *(Torta Paradiso)*

1 cup plus 2 tablespoons unsalted butter, softened
1 1/3 cups superfine granulated sugar
5 large egg yolks at room temperature
5 large eggs at room temperature
1 2/3 cups all-purpose unbleached flour
1 1/2 cups potato starch flour
1 teaspoon baking powder
1/2 teaspoon salt
Grated rind of 1 1/2 lemons
Grated rind of 1/2 orange
1 teaspoon vanilla extract
Confectioner's sugar

1. Preheat oven to 350 degrees.
2. Cream the butter and granulated sugar together until soft and fluffy.
3. Beat the egg yolks until light in color. Add the whole eggs and beat for at least 10 minutes with the electric mixer or 2 minutes with a whisk as the final texture of the cake depends on long beating.
4. Add the beaten eggs, about a tablespoon at a time, to the butter and sugar. Mix in with a spoon.
5. When all the eggs are incorporated in the butter-sugar mixture, sift the flours, baking powder, and salt together 3 times; then add them to the egg mixture about 1/2 cup at a time, folding in with a spoon or spatula after each addition.
6. Add the fruit rind and vanilla.
7. Butter a 12-inch spring-form pan, cut a circle of waxed paper to line the bottom, and butter it once it is in place. Pour the batter into the pan, tilting the pan to make sure of even distribution.
8. Bake in a moderate (350-degree) oven for about 1 hour or until the cake is risen high and is golden brown on top and a cake tester comes out clean.
9. Allow to cool in pan, then turn out on a serving plate, peel off the waxed paper and sprinkle generously with sifted or sieved confectioner's sugar. Or you may make patterns on top of the cake by cutting out designs in waxed paper to fit the top, then sprinkling sugar over all and lifting away the waxed paper. Paradise Cake is excellent with a dessert wine or champagne. It keeps superbly, and its flavor approaches its best 24 hours after baking.

Makes 1 (12-inch) cake

Irene Rothschild is the hostess of the WCAU "Kitchen," and has been teaching cooking classes throughout the Delaware Valley for many years. She currently offers culinary classes at Temple University and is the editor of *The Easy Gourmet Cookbook*. Ms. Rothschild created a special midmorning coffee-break as part of a larger brunch at Americus restaurant in the Society Hill Sheraton on March 20, 1988.

The Society Hill section of Philadelphia received a real boost when the Sheraton Hotel opened there a few years ago. Tourists and residents enter the lovely atrium lobby where afternoon tea is served. One of the hotel's finest features is Americus, known for its steaks and seafood. The restaurant also specializes in elegant and elaborate Sunday brunch.

The bi-level dining room has comfortable upholstered chairs, softly colored walls, and fresh flowers. Guests enjoy a bottle of California Chardonnay or Cabernet Sauvignon from the fine wine list.

Entrees include prime New York Strip Loin, Filet Mignon, and Roasted Prime Rib of Beef, all served with Bourbon Glazed Onions and Sautéed Mushrooms with a choice of bearnaise or peppercorn sauce. Rack of lamb, veal, and Long Island duck served with fresh strawberries and Grand Marnier are also available.

TIA MARIA BANANA BREAD

DRAMBUIE CHEESE LOG

TIA MARIA FRENCH TOAST

French Roast Coffee and Orange Pekoe Tea

Serves 8

TIA MARIA BANANA BREAD

1 1/2 cups all-purpose flour
2 teaspoons baking soda
1/2 pound butter
2 cups sugar
2 cups mashed ripe banana
4 eggs
1/4 cup Tia Maria
1 cup pecan pieces

1. Combine all ingredients in a mixing bowl. Blend well. Pour mixture into a greased 9-inch x 5-inch loaf pan. Bake in a 350-degree oven 60 to 70 minutes.

Serve with Drambuie Cheese Log

Makes 1 loaf

DRAMBUIE CHEESE LOG

10 ounces mild goat cheese
8 ounces cream cheese
3 tablespoons Drambuie
1/2 orange, rind grated

1. Bring cheeses to room temperature. Place in food processor fitted with steel blade, or blender, or in bowl of mixer. Blend well. Add Drambuie and orange rind. Orange juice may be added for extra flavor. Blend.
2. Form into log and wrap in plastic wrap. Chill until serving time. Serve with crackers or Tia Maria Banana Bread.

Makes 1 log

TIA MARIA FRENCH TOAST

8 large eggs
2 cups milk
2 tablespoons sugar
Pinch salt
1 tablespoon ground cinnamon
1/2 cup Tia Maria
3 cups Sugar Frosted Flakes
1/2 cup sliced almonds, chopped
Butter for cooking French toast
1 loaf cinnamon raisin bread

1. Combine eggs, milk, sugar, salt, cinnamon, and Tia Maria in a large bowl. Crush the Frosted Flakes and the almonds together in another bowl.
2. Dip the bread in the egg mixture and let it soak through. Coat the soaked bread in the cereal and nut mixture.
3. Cook the French toast in melted butter on a griddle until it is golden brown and the inside is almost the consistency of custard.

Serve with butter and maple syrup.

Elisabeth Rozin is an educator, lecturer, and culinary consultant who believes in the universal pleasure of good food. She has lived in Mexico and France and has incorporated the flavors of these nations and others in *Ethnic Cuisine: The Flavor Principle Cookbook*. Her articles have appeared in *Natural History*, *Appetite*, and *Professional Nutritionist*. Rozin lives in Havertown, Pennsylvania where she is currently at work on her latest cookbook, "Blue Corn and Chocolate."

She and chef/proprietor Jude Erwin prepared this meal with recipes from *Ethnic Cuisine*, at Serrano on March 17 and 18, 1988.

Rick Machlin and Jude Erwin named their restaurant after serrano chile, the spicy ingredient that turns up in drinks and dishes from martinis to Indonesian specials. Serrano, located in Olde City not far from Society Hill, has a casual, friendly atmosphere. The bar lines one side of the restaurant which has exposed brick walls and a fireplace. Machlin serves as bartender and recommends a variety of drinks from vodka with saffron or hot peppers to the latest domestic and imported beer.

Erwin oversees the kitchen which produces an eclectic mix from American burgers to Middle Eastern dishes, such as Baba Ghanouj with Pita. Through the years, the restaurant has offered an authentic Indonesian Rijstafel, Spanish Paella, and Portuguese meals.

AFRICAN PEANUT CHICKEN SOUP

INDONESIAN CUCUMBER SALAD

CASSOULET

VANILLA ICE CREAM WITH CHILI-GINGER SAUCE

Dry Vodka Martini with Saffron

Serves 8

AFRICAN PEANUT CHICKEN SOUP

2 medium onions, chopped
2 large red and/or green peppers, chopped
3 to 4 cloves garlic, mashed
2 tablespoons oil
1 (28-ounce) can tomatoes, coarsely chopped
8 cups chicken stock
1/4 teaspoon pepper
1/4 teaspoon crushed hot red peppers
1/2 cup rice
1 to 1 1/2 cups cooked chicken, chopped
2/3 cup smooth, unflavored (no salt or sugar) peanut butter

1. In a large pot, sauté onions, peppers, and garlic in oil over moderate to high heat until onions are just beginning to brown.
2. Add all other ingredients except rice, chicken and peanut butter and simmer, uncovered, over low heat for about 1 hour.
3. Add rice and chicken and simmer for about 15 to 20 minutes or until rice is tender. Add peanut butter and mix or whisk until it is completely dissolved and smooth. Heat to a simmer and serve.

NOTE: Leftover soup will keep well in freezer for up to three months.

INDONESIAN CUCUMBER SALAD

4 cucumbers
2 carrots
2 scallions, finely chopped
1 teaspoon salt
1 clove garlic, finely minced
2 teaspoons ginger root, finely minced
1 1/2 teaspoons tumeric
Pinch crushed dried red peppers
1/3 cup water
1/4 cup distilled white vinegar
1/4 cup sugar

1. Peel cucumbers and cut into narrow strips, discarding center pulp and seeds. Cut carrots into narrow strips.
2. Combine scallions, salt, garlic, ginger root, tumeric, red peppers, and water. Simmer over low heat 10 minutes. Remove from heat, add vinegar and sugar, mix well and pour over cucumber and carrot strips.
3. Marinate several hours or overnight in refrigerator. Serve chilled.

CASSOULET

1 pound dried white beans (Great Northern or marrow)
4 whole cloves
1 medium onion, peeled
1/4 teaspoon freshly ground black pepper
1 carrot, sliced
1/4 cup parsley, chopped
1 stalk celery with leaves, chopped
1 tablespoon salt
1/2 pound bulk sausage meat
1 stalk celery with leaves, chopped
1 tablespoon salt
1/2 pound garlic or Polish sausage, sliced
1 cup diced cooked pork
1 cup diced cooked poultry (duck, goose, turkey, or chicken)
1 medium onion, chopped
2 cloves garlic, mashed
1/2 cup dry white wine
1 (8-ounce) can tomato sauce
2 teaspoons thyme
1 teaspoon dried basil
1/4 cup butter
1/2 cup dry bread crumbs
1/3 cup parsley, chopped

1. Soak beans overnight in enough cold water to cover. Drain.
2. Stick 2 cloves in each end of the onion. Place the onion, beans, pepper, carrots, parsley, and celery in a large pot; pour in about 2 quarts cold water. Simmer uncovered over low heat about 1 1/2 to 2 hours or until beans are tender. Add 1 tablespoon salt for last 1/2 hour of cooking.
3. Drain beans, reserving cooking liquid, which should measure about 1 1/2 to 2 cups. Discard clove-studded onion.
4. In a large frying pan, brown sausage meat and sausage slices. Remove from pan. Mix in pork and poultry, and set aside.
5. Drain all but 1 tablespoon fat from pan. Add chopped onion and garlic, and sauté until golden. Add wine, tomato sauce, 1/2 teaspoon salt, pepper, thyme, and basil, then add reserved bean liquid. Cook uncovered over low heat for about 15 minutes, scraping up all brown bits from bottom of pan. You should have about 2 cups of sauce.

6. In a deep casserole, alternate layers of beans and combined mixed meats. Pour sauce into casserole.
7. In a small frying pan melt butter, add bread crumbs and parsley and sauté, stirring, for a few minutes.
8. Spread bread crumb mixture evenly over the top of the casserole. Cover and bake in a preheated 350-degree oven for about 1 hour. Remove cover for last 10 minutes of baking.

Vanilla Ice Cream with Chili-Ginger Sauce

2 cups sugar
2 cups water
3 tablespoons pickled Japanese ginger, finely shredded
1/4 cup dried apricots, chopped
1/4 cup raisins
1/4 cup slivered almonds
1/4 cup chopped walnuts
Splash of grenadine
Dash hot red pepper, or to taste
Vanilla ice cream

1. Combine sugar and water in a saucepan. Simmer for 15 minutes to make a simple syrup.
2. Add remaining ingredients and simmer 5 more minutes.
3. Serve over vanilla ice cream.

Makes approximately 2 1/2 cups. Sauce will keep for a long period of time if kept in a covered container in the refrigerator.

Pastry chef Nancy Silverton, a Los Angeles native, studied and mastered her art at the Cordon Bleu school in London and Ecole Lenotre in Plaisir-grignon, France. She is a protégé of Maida Heatter who feels Silverton is "following in her footsteps."

Silverton has created pastries, tarts, tea loaves, and cookies at Michael's, Spago, and Chinois on Main in California and Maxwell's Plum in New York, where she now makes her home. Confections from her book *Desserts* were served at Le Beau Lieu at The Barclay Hotel during a coffee-hour on March 17, 1988.

Its name means "the beautiful place," and Le Beau Lieu is housed in The Barclay, one of Philadelphia's most beautiful hotels, just steps away from Rittenhouse Square. Everything about Le Beau Lieu is strictly French, from Maitre d' Pierre Pim, who greets you at the door, to the classic cuisine carefully prepared by Chef Gilbert Guinoiseau.

The dining room is quietly elegant, set off by fresh flowers, linen, crystal, and silver. The atmosphere is conducive to studying the a la carte menu and wine list. Here diners feast on smoked salmon or foie gras with a glass of sauterne, cool vichyssoise or a salad of baby greens accented with chevre and perhaps accompanied with a chilled Chablis. Entrees include Florida pompano, sole, swordfish, roast rack of lamb, veal, and ragout of chicken and lobster tail.

A cheese course is offered before dessert. The cheese goes well with the fine wines available at Le Beau Lieu. Although the food is French, the restaurant specializes in American vintages.

CHOCOLATE TERRINE WITH BUTTER CHOCOLATE GLAZE

CHOCOLATE MINT COOKIES

ESPRESSO LOAF

Coffee

Serves 10

CHOCOLATE TERRINE WITH BUTTER CHOCOLATE GLAZE

For the Terrine:
1 tablespoon unsalted butter, melted, to prepare pan
18 ounces bittersweet chocolate, cut in 2-inch pieces
6 ounces unsalted butter (1 1/2 sticks)
12 egg yolks
5 tablespoons granulated sugar, divided
3/4 cup heavy cream
2 tablespoons sour cream
3 egg whites
For the Glaze:
8 ounces bittersweet chocolate, cut in 2-inch pieces
6 tablespoons unsalted butter (3/4 stick)
1 tablespoon plus 1 teaspoon light corn syrup
3/4 cup heavy cream
6 tablespoons cognac (or alcohol of your choice)
3 tablespoons unsweetened cocoa powder (optional if your chocolate is not bitter enough)

1. Prepare a 10 x 4-inch foil-covered cardboard rectangle to unmold the terrine onto.
2. Using the terrine mold as a guide, cut out parchment or wax paper pieces to fit bottom, ends and sides of a slant-sided French 10 x 4-inch terrine mold with 3-inch sides. (A loaf pan, used for baking bread, can also be used, but it will hold only about 4 cups.) This recipe yields 6 cups of chocolate mixture. Brush the mold with melted butter and line with paper. Set aside.
3. In a heatproof bowl, melt chocolate with 6 ounces butter over barely simmering water. (The water should not touch the bottom of the bowl or the chocolate will burn.) Turn off heat and let stand over warm water until ready to use.
4. Using the whisk attachment of an electric mixer, beat together the egg yolks and 4 tablespoons sugar on high speed until the mixture is thick and mousse-like. Gradually whisk chocolate mixture into egg yolk mixture, then return it to the heatproof bowl.
5. Over gently simmering water, whisk a few minutes until mixture is thick, shiny, and the whisk leaves an empty trail behind when it is drawn across the bottom of the pan. Remove from heat, set aside for a few minutes to cool.
6. Using the whisk attachment of an electric mixer, beat the heavy cream with the sour cream on low speed until it thickens enough not to spatter. Increase speed to medium high and beat

until thick and mousse-like. Remove from mixer. Whisk a few times by hand until soft peaks form. Whisk the whipped cream into the chocolate mixture.

7. Beat the egg whites on low speed until frothy. Increase speed to medium and beat until soft peaks form. Increase speed to high and gradually beat in remaining tablespoon of sugar, until stiff, glossy peaks form. It is important that the egg whites be beaten completely smooth before they are incorporated into the chocolate or there will be little white specks in the terrine.
8. Whisk 1/3 of the egg whites into the chocolate mixture, then fold in the rest. Pour mixture into the terrine mold, smooth the top and chill. You can freeze the terrine for no more than 1 1/2 hours or place in refrigerator for at least 5 hours.
9. To prepare glaze, melt chocolate with butter and corn syrup over barely simmering water. (The water should not touch the bottom of the bowl or the chocolate will burn.) Turn off heat and let mixture stand over warm water until ready to use.
10. In a small saucepan whisk together the cream, cognac, and cocoa powder. Bring to a simmer over medium heat, whisking constantly until the cocoa powder is dissolved. Scrape into the melted chocolate mixture and stir to combine.
11. Before unmolding terrine, spread 3 to 4 tablespoons warm glaze in a very thin layer on top to form a barrier that will keep it from sticking to the serving platter. Return to freezer or refrigerator until the chocolate layer hardens.
12. Unmold terrine and pour or ladle the warm glaze over length of the terrine, allowing glaze to flow over the top and sides in a thin layer, making an even coating. Return to refrigerator or freezer for 45 minutes until glaze is firm.

Makes 1 (10 x 4-inch) terrine

Espresso Loaf Cake

1 tablespoon unsalted butter, melted
2/3 cup plus 1 tablespoon pastry flour, divided
3 tablespoons unsalted butter
1/2 cup almond meal
1/2 teaspoon baking powder
3 tablespoons ground coffee
7 egg yolks
1 1/2 tablespoons grated or finely chopped lemon zest (1 lemon)
3/4 cup granulated sugar, divided
2 tablespoons instant coffee
10 egg whites

1. Preheat oven to 350 degrees. Adjust rack to top third of oven. Brush a 12 x 3 x 3-inch straight-sided French terrine mold (8-cup capacity) with half of melted butter and line the bottom with paper. Butter again and chill briefly to set. Dust the pan with 1 tablespoon of flour and knock out excess; set aside.
2. Melt the butter in a small saucepan and set aside in a warm place. Sift together the remaining pastry flour, almond meal, baking powder, and ground coffee; set aside. If any coffee grounds or almond meal remain in the strainer, stir them back into the flour mixture.
3. In a heatproof bowl (preferably the bowl of an electric mixer), whisk together the egg yolks, lemon zest, 1/2 cup sugar and the instant coffee. Place over a pot of gently simmering water and lightly whisk together until the mixture is warm to the touch (about 100 degrees). Place bowl on mixer.
4. Using the whisk attachment, beat briefly on high speed to release heat and then reduce speed to medium and beat until the mixture has tripled in volume, is thick and mousse-like and the outside of the bowl is cool to the touch. Take a few tablespoons of batter and whisk it into the melted butter. Return this small portion back to the batter and whisk together to combine; set aside.
5. Using the electric attachment of an electric mixer, beat the egg whites on low speed until frothy. Increase speed to medium and beat until soft peaks form. Increase speed to high and very gradually beat in the remaining 1/4 cup sugar, beating until stiff, glossy peaks form.
6. Pour the mixture on top of the yolks but do not mix them in. Then whisk about 1/3 of the egg whites into the bowl, whisking until well mixed. Fold in the remaining egg whites, combining well. Work quickly. Once the ground coffee has been added to

7. the batter the acid in it can break down the batter and make it runny. Turn 1/2 of the batter into each end of the prepared pan, letting it run naturally into the center of the pan. Do not level off. (Having a "valley" in the center of the loaf pan will create a cake without a hump in the center and will discourage cracking.)
8. Bake 15 minutes until the surface is set, then prop open the oven door slightly and continue to bake for 35 to 40 minutes more until the cake is springy to the touch and shrinks away from the sides of the pan. For a firm, solid cake that slices well, cool completely before unmolding. Leftover cake freezes well.

Makes 1 loaf for 8

CHOCOLATE MINT COOKIES

12 ounces bittersweet chocolate, cut into 2-inch pieces
4 tablespoons unsalted butter (1/2 stick)
6 tablespoons crème de menthe or peppermint schnapps
1/2 cup fresh mint leaves (preferably spearmint), chopped
1 cup almond meal
1/2 cup plus 2 tablespoons flour
3/4 teaspoon baking powder
3 eggs
1/2 cup granulated sugar
To Coat Cookies:
3/4 cup granulated sugar
3/4 cup sifted powdered sugar

1. In a heatproof bowl, melt the chocolate with butter over barely simmering water. (The water should not touch the bottom of the bowl or the chocolate will burn.) Turn off heat and let mixture stand over warm water until ready to use.
2. In a small saucepan, scald the crème de menthe with chopped mint leaves. Remove from heat, cover and let stand approximately 15 minutes.
3. In a bowl, stir together the almond meal, flour and baking powder. Sift through strainer to remove any lumps. If any almond meal remains in the strainer, stir it back into the flour to recombine; set aside.
4. Using the whisk attachment of an electric mixer, beat the eggs at high speed with 1/2 cup granulated sugar until the mixture is thick, pale and forms a ribbon when the beater is lifted out of the bowl, about 5 minutes.
5. Pour the crème de menthe into the chocolate mixture and stir to combine. Whisk the chocolate mixture into the egg mixture until combined. Whisk in the flour mixture, combining well. The batter will be runny. Chill batter until very solid, at least 4 hours.
6. Preheat the oven to 325 degrees. Adjust the oven rack to the middle position. Work with the dough in small batches, keeping the rest refrigerated.
7. With your hands, roll the dough into 1-inch balls and place on a baking sheet. (Your hands are bound to get a bit messy - I usually have to wash my hands several times while making these.) Chill until firm, 10 to 15 minutes.
8. The unusual white color of these cookies is achieved by rolling them first in granulated sugar and then in powdered sugar before baking. The granulated sugar acts as a barrier to prevent the

butter in the cookies from melting the powdered sugar so they stay very white.

9. To coat the cookies, place 3/4 cup granulated sugar and 3/4 cup sifted powdered sugar in 2 small bowls. Remove cookies from refrigerator and roll 1 at a time in the bowl of granulated sugar to lightly coat. Then place in the bowl of powdered sugar and coat them heavily. The cookies must be completely white.

   If the dark chocolate color bleeds through before baking, roll again in powdered sugar. Place on paper-lined or nonstick baking sheet 1 1/2 inches apart.

10. Bake for 20 minutes. Remove from oven as soon as the cookies can be lifted off the baking sheet without sticking. Allow to cool completely. The cookies will remain soft in the center and will be white with 2 or 3 dark chocolate cracks.

Don't stack these cookies to store or you'll loosen the powdered sugar coating.

Makes 3 dozen

Since Philadelphia is a city of neighborhoods, Irina Smith and Ann Hazan visited many ethnic communities, including outlying areas. They interviewed the people who make the neighborhoods great and asked for their recipes. The result is *The Original Philadelphia Neighborhood Cookbook*, a cultural culinary journey through the city streets. Irina Smith is the co-author of *To Market, To Market: Philadelphia's Italian Market* and *To Market, To Market: Philadelphia's Reading Terminal Market*. Ann Hazan teaches cooking classes at Temple University.

This dinner was presented at Vinh Hoa, a Vietnamese restaurant in South Philadelphia, on March 20, 1988. The Spring Roll recipe is from *The Original Philadelphia Neighborhood Cookbook*. The main courses are the creation of Chef Anh Phungly.

Vinh Hoa, situated in the center of South Philadelphia, is one of many restaurants serving Southeast Asian cuisine in what is still a strongly Italian-American neighborhood. The restaurant is decorated with bamboo mats, ornamental batiks on the ceiling, and a colorful fish tank. The room is softly lit by candlelight, and tables are arranged to encourage family dinners.

Chef Anh Phungly presents the classic Vietnamese dishes for which her country is famous. They are accented with lemon grass and sweet and sour sauces. Starters include Spring Rolls and Shrimp Toast, a puff pastry filled with ground shrimp and served with a sweet dipping sauce. Classic soups include Corn and Crab, and Beef and Rice Stick.

A wide variety of fish, beef, fowl, and pork dishes appear on the menu including Crispy Duck, Chicken and Shrimp with Lemon Grass sautée, Satays of Beef, Chicken or Pork with Caramel Sauce, and the famous Vietnamese Pancakes. Desserts include the traditional Flan or Green Tapioca Custard.

Vinh Hoa has a fine selection of wines and beer from many lands, including China and Korea.

MENU

SPRING ROLLS

(Cha Ctio)

CHICKEN WITH PINEAPPLE AND SAVORY LEAVES

(Cia Xai Thom Va La Que)

BEEF WITH FIVE SPICES

(Bo Xao Ngu U Huong)

FRESH FRUIT IN SEASON

Beer

Serves 4

SPRING ROLLS *(Cha Ctio)*

For Spring Rolls:
1 pound ground lean pork
1 large onion, finely chopped
4 ounces cellophane noodles, soaked in warm water 3 minutes then cut into 1-inch strips
2 ounces wood-ears, soaked in warm water 15 minutes, cleaned and finely chopped
1 teaspoon salt
1/2 teaspoon black pepper
2 tablespoons fish sauce (available at Oriental markets)
1 tablespoon dry sherry
4 extra large eggs
1/2 pound fresh bean sprouts
8 large rice paper circles
Soybean oil for deep-frying, about 2 cups
For the Nuoc Cham Sauce:
1/2 cup fish sauce
1 1/2 cups water
5 teaspoons vinegar
1/4 to 1/2 cup sugar
1/4 cup grated carrot
1 teaspoon chili pepper flakes

1. Prepare nuoc cham sauce. Combine all ingredients until well blended and set aside.
2. To make the filling, combine pork, onion, noodles, wood-ears, salt, pepper, fish sauce, and sherry. Lightly beat 1 of the eggs and add to mixture. Mix in bean sprouts.
3. Cut each rice paper circle into 3-inch pie-shaped wedges. Beat remaining 3 eggs and brush each triangle with egg before adding filling. Place 2 to 3 tablespoons of filling on each triangle at the pointed end. Fold end over filling, fold sides in, then roll firmly. Press edges together to seal.
4. Heat oil to 350 degrees for frying. Fry rolls a few at a time until lightly browned and filling is cooked through, about 12 minutes. Drain on paper towels. Serve with nuoc cham sauce.

Variation: Garlic and chopped shrimp may be added to filling if desired.

Makes about 24

NOTE: Leftover cooked Spring Rolls will keep in the freezer. Reheat in the microwave or conventional oven.

CHICKEN WITH PINEAPPLE AND SAVORY LEAVES *(Cia Xai Thom Va La Que)*

1 pound chicken breast, skinned, sliced into 1-inch-wide strips
2 scallions, white portion only, finely chopped, divided
4 garlic cloves, minced, divided
2 teaspoons salt
2 teaspoons sugar
2 tablespoons bottled fish sauce
1 teaspoon white pepper
2 tablespoons dry sherry
6 tablespoons soybean oil
1 fresh pineapple, peeled, cored and quartered, then cut into 1/4-inch thick slices (unsweetened canned pineapple may be used)
1/3 cup chicken broth (canned may be used), divided
2 teaspoons cornstarch dissolved in 1/4 cup water
40 savory leaves, finely chop 30, reserve 10 for garnish

1. Place chicken strips on a plate. Add 1/2 each of the minced scallions and garlic. Add salt, sugar, and fish sauce, and mix well. Add white pepper and dry sherry, and mix thoroughly.
2. In a skillet, heat soybean oil until hot. Add remaining scallions and cook, stirring constantly, for 1 minute. Add remaining garlic and cook 1 more minute.
3. Add chicken to skillet and cook 1 minute, stirring frequently. Add pineapple and 1/2 of the chicken broth. Cook 1 minute. Add remaining broth, cover skillet and cook for 3 to 5 minutes or until chicken is done. Do not overcook chicken.
4. Stir in cornstarch mixture and cook for 1 minute.
5. Remove skillet from heat and stir in chopped savory. Place chicken with pineapple on serving platter and garnish with savory leaves. Serve at once.

BEEF WITH FIVE SPICES
(Bo Xao Ngu U Huong)

1 pound flank steak, thinly sliced
2 scallions, white portion only, finely chopped, divided
6 garlic cloves, mashed then minced, divided
1 tablespoon light soy sauce
1 tablespoon bottled fish sauce
1 teaspoon salt
2 teaspoons sugar
2 stalks lemon grass, finely chopped
2 tablespoons Sake
1 teaspoon white pepper
1/4 teaspoon five-spice powder
6 tablespoons soybean oil
1/2 cup chicken broth (canned may be used)
2 teaspoons cornstarch mixed with 1/4 cup water
1 large cucumber, sliced into rounds for garnish
1 hot red pepper, thinly sliced for garnish

1. Place sliced beef on a plate. Add 1/2 each of the minced scallion and garlic. Add the soy, fish sauce, salt, sugar, 2 tablespoons lemon grass, Sake, white pepper, and five-spice powder. Combine thoroughly.
2. In a skillet, heat oil over medium-high heat. Add remaining scallion and garlic and cook 1 minute.
3. Add beef and stir-fry quickly for 2 minutes. Stir in chicken broth and remaining lemon grass. Add cornstarch mixture and cook 30 seconds. Remove skillet from heat.
4. Surround a platter with cucumber slices. Add beef and top with hot red pepper slices. Serve at once.

Louis Szathmary was the owner of The Bakery Restaurant on Chicago's Near North Side. Trained as a journalist in his native Hungary, this multi-talented man has enjoyed acting and lecturing throughout the world. He is a member of numerous culinary associations and the author of five books including *The Bakery Restaurant Cookbook*.

Szathmary and Chef/proprietor Fritz Blank of Deux Cheminées prepared this French dinner on March 27, 1987. The recipes for the soup and dessert can be found in *The Bakery Restaurant Cookbook*. The main course is Fritz Blank's creation.

In French, *deux cheminées* means two fireplaces, and two fireplaces were the focal points of Chef Fritz Blank's restaurant until a fire in the kitchen necessitated a move to the restaurant's present location not far from Philadelphia's theater district. The new Deux Cheminées is housed in the old Princeton Club. The restaurant has several magnificent rooms where the decor is as fine as the cuisine. There are high ceilings, softly painted walls set off with fine art, fireplaces which bring warmth and romance in colder months, and 18th and 19th century furnishings.

The menu is prix fixe and the dishes reflect Blank's style. His cuisine centers on the freshest ingredients, simply prepared in the French style. Soups are made from the clearest stocks, salads are composed of tender, lightly dressed greens, and main courses change with the seasons.

The wine list is superb and Blank suggests that to accompany fish, a fine Chardonnay fills the bill nicely.

CREAM OF KOHLRABI SOUP

(Crème au Chou-Rave)

TWO FISH WITH TWO SAUCES

(Deux Poissons aux Deux Sauces)

BUTTERED BABY CARROTS

(Petite Carottes)

STEAMED RICE

(Riz)

APPLE STRUDEL

Macon Chardonnay

Cream of Kohlrabi Soup
(Crème au Chou-Rave)

2 tablespoons shortening, preferably lard
1/2 cup chopped onion
1 small carrot, scraped
1 cup chopped celery
1 tablespoon sugar
4 cups peeled kohlrabi heads, cut into 1/2-inch dice
2 tablespoons chopped fresh parsley
2 quarts veal stock; chicken stock; or enough canned chicken broth, diluted, to make 2 quarts
1 cheesecloth bag filled with 1/2 teaspoon peppercorns, 1/2 bay leaf, and 1 teaspoon dried tarragon
1 tablespoon salt, divided
4 tablespoons butter
6 tablespoons flour
2 cups milk
1 cup half-and-half
1 cup sour cream, at room temperature

1. In a large pot, melt shortening. Add the chopped onion and cook, stirring constantly, over medium heat until the onion starts to turn yellow. Add carrot and celery and cook another 2 minutes, continuing to stir. Add sugar, kohlrabi and 1 tablespoon chopped parsley. Cover and cook over very low heat, stirring occasionally. Be sure ingredients do not stick to bottom of the pot. Cook for 15 minutes.
2. Add the stock of your choice, the cheesecloth bag and 1/2 the salt.
3. Bring the soup to a boil over medium heat. Reduce the heat and simmer.
4. In a small saucepan, melt the butter. Mix the flour into the milk with a wire whip and slowly, stirring constantly with the wire whip, add the flour-milk mixture to the butter. If you add it slowly enough, it will thicken immediately and when you finish you will have a white sauce of medium consistency.
5. Remove from heat and dilute with the half-and-half. Pour this mixture into the simmering soup. Stir gently with a wooden spoon and let simmer another 15 to 20 minutes. Check for seasoning and add a little more salt if necessary. (The amount will depend on the saltiness of the stock used.)
6. Just before serving, place the sour cream in the soup tureen. Mix in the remaining chopped fresh parsley. Put 2 or 3 ladles of hot

soup into the tureen and stir it into the sour cream. Remove cheesecloth bag and pour all the soup into the tureen.

NOTE: Leftover soup will keep in the refrigerator for 2 days or prepare the recipe through step 3 and freeze the amount of soup which will not be served right away.

TWO FISH WITH TWO SAUCES
(Deux Poissons aux Deux Sauces)

1 1/2 pounds fillet of black bass, skin removed, cut into finger-size pieces
1 1/2 pounds fillet of salmon, skin removed, cut into 1/4- inch medallions
Water
Juice of 1/2 lemon
Salt
For the Red Wine Sauce (Vin Rouge):
3 to 4 carrots, cut into 1-inch pieces
2 shallots, roughly chopped
1 medium-small onion, roughly chopped
1 cup dry red wine
1/2 cup port
1 quart fish fumet
1 pint mussel juice
10 to 12 mussels
10 to 12 scallops
1 small bouquet garni
2 to 3 tablespoons beef demiglacé
1 small piece coating chocolate, about the size of a lima bean
1 tablespoon cornstarch dissolved in 1 cup water
2 tablespoons unsalted butter
Salt, pepper and lemon juice, optional
For the White Wine Sauce (Beurre Blanc):
1 cup dry white wine or vermouth
1/3 cup white wine vinegar
1/3 cup shallots, chopped
2 1/4 cups heavy cream
1/2 pound unsalted butter, cut into 1-inch cubes
Salt and white pepper to taste
Few drops lemon juice
Freshly chopped herbs, optional

1. To make the red wine sauce, sauté the carrots, shallots and onion in a sauté pan until the onions sweat. Adjust heat to high and add red wine and port. Bring to a full boil and ignite to burn off the alcohol.
2. When the flame dies, add the fish fumet, mussel juice, mussels, scallops, and bouquet garni. Bring to a boil and adjust heat to a gentle simmer. Reduce the liquid by 1/2. Pass through a sieve.

3. Add beef demiglacé and coating chocolate. Stir to incorporate then thicken very slightly (just to coat a spoon) with cornstarch-water mixture). Pass again through a sieve. Finish with 2 tablespoons unsalted butter. Season with salt and pepper and a few drops of lemon juice, if desired.

To prepare the Fish:

1. Gently poach the black bass fillets in a fish poacher or in a sauté pan filled with water to cover. Simmer gently for 10 minutes. Remove to a warm platter and cover with foil.
2. Do the same with the salmon.
3. On each of 4 serving plates, evenly divide the bass and salmon. Top the bass with white wine sauce and the salmon with the red wine sauce. Or, for a different presentation, divide each plate in half and place a pool of each sauce side-by-side. Top with fish.

APPLE STRUDEL

For the Dough:
3 cups flour
Pinch salt
1 1/2 tablespoons lard
1 medium egg
1 teaspoon plain white vinegar
1 to 1 1/4 cups lukewarm water
1 tablespoon farina
For the Filling:
3 pounds apples, peeled and cored (winesap apples are recommended, but tart varieties like pie apples or greenings are also good), grated
1 cup sugar, approximately, depending on the sweetness of the apples
1/2 cup white raisins, soaked in hot water, patted dry, optional
Pinch cinnamon
1/2 cup breadcrumbs
1/2 cup ground almonds

1. Sift the flour onto a pastry board into a cone shape. Make a well in the middle and place in the well the salt, lard, egg, vinegar and a little bit of lukewarm water. With your fingertips, start to work all the soft ingredients into the flour, adding small amounts of water until you make the whole flour into a mass. First it will be sticky, but as you work, it will turn very elastic with air bubbles inside.
2. Form the dough into a ball, sprinkle a corner of the pastry board with a very little flour, place the ball on it, pat it down somewhat and with your fingertips brush the top with a very small amount of lard. Then cover the ball with a saucepan that has been warmed over medium heat.
3. Let it stand for 20 to 25 minutes, or even longer. Have all your fillings ready at hand before you start to work with the dough. Cover a large table with a tablecloth, dust the tablecloth with 3 to 4 tablespoons flour mixed with 1 tablespoon farina.
4. Now, with your fingers, brush the dough with a little bit of lard, and start to pull it first to the left, then to the right. After a little pulling, go under the dough with your fist and try to pull it over your fist from the middle towards the 2 edges at once. If the dough is good, it will start to get thin. Then, holding it very gently with your fingers and being very careful not to make a hole in it with your fingernails, start to lift and pull the dough all over the table, walking around in one direction. You have to use the kind of waving movement that you would use

to straighten a blanket over a bed. Pull the dough until it is large enough that it hangs off the table all around. Cut off the excess hanging dough and let the thin strudel dough dry for 10 minutes or so.

5. Now start the filling. Melt 1/2 cup unsalted butter and sprinkle the surface of the dough with the butter. Then sprinkle the whole surface with about 1/2 cup of the dry fine breadcrumbs mixed with 1/2 cup ground almonds or ground walnuts. Let grated apples stand 15 to 30 minutes and press through a sieve to release juice. Mix with sugar, cinnamon and raisins.
6. Spread the apple filling on about 1/3 of the strudel dough. Holding the tablecloth, start to roll the strudel dough, including the filling, by moving the tablecloth so that the strudel starts to roll up jelly-roll fashion. Keep sprinkling with melted butter as it turns, and keep rolling until the whole dough is rolled up. Now cut the strudel into the length of your cookie sheet, brush the cookie sheet and the top of the strudel with melted butter and transfer the strudel to the cookie sheet with a long metal spatula or a long knife.
7. Bake in a very hot oven 25 to 45 minutes, depending on the amount and kind of strudel.

In 1961, First Lady Jacqueline Kennedy met René Verdon at New York's posh La Caravelle. She was so impressed with his talent, she asked him to become Executive Chef at the White House. Verdon, who grew up around Marseilles, is the author of *The White House Chef Cookbook* and *The Enlightened Cuisine*.

Although Verdon says "haute cuisine is in my blood," he utilizes the techniques and classic dishes of French cuisine to create new recipes with a contemporary, California flair. His newest book is *Convection Cuisine*, which he wrote with Jacqueline Mallorca.

Verdon created this dinner with Chef Miro Loeffler of Between Friends, located in the Wyndham Franklin Plaza Hotel, on March 17 and 18, 1989. All recipes can be found in *Convection Cuisine*.

Between Friends is the plush luxurious restaurant of the Wyndham Franklin Plaza Hotel. It is located near the Logan Square section of the city. Its damask white linen and crystal are illuminated by gentle candlelight. The menu features a mixture of French dishes with California cuisine. A fine variety of wines from around the world are featured.

RED SNAPPER WRAPPED IN ZUCCHINI

QUAIL WITH CRACKED CORIANDER AND WILTED SPINACH SALAD

SAUTÉED RED AND YELLOW PEPPER STRIPS

HAZELNUT MERINGUE AND CHOCOLATE CREAM GATEAU

Dry Creek Fumé Blanc, 1986
Cain Cellars Merlot, 1982
Serves 4

RED SNAPPER WRAPPED IN ZUCCHINI

1 clove garlic, chopped
1 (8-ounce) fillet of red snapper
Salt and pepper
Paprika
2 small zucchini, about 4 ounces each
1 tablespoon olive oil
1/4 cup dry white wine
1 teaspoon chopped fresh thyme leaves, or 1/2 teaspoon dried thyme leaves mixed with 1/2 teaspoon fresh chopped parsley
1/4 cup heavy cream

1. Preheat convection oven to 375 degrees. Grease a shallow baking dish and sprinkle with garlic.
2. Remove any stray bones from snapper, sprinkle with salt, pepper, and paprika to taste. Cut the fish into 8 equal pieces.
3. Cut zucchini lengthwise into paper-thin slices. (An easy way to do this is to lay the zucchini flat, trim one end, and shave off slices with a wide-bladed vegetable peeler.) If the slices are not almost transparent, blanch them in boiling water for a few seconds to make them pliable.
4. Place 2 zucchini slices, overlapping, on a work surface. Put a piece of fish on one end, and roll up the fish in the zucchini. Repeat with remaining fish and zucchini. Lay rolls in prepared baking dish and sprinkle with olive oil, wine, thyme, salt, pepper, and paprika to taste. (Dish can be prepared ahead to this point, covered, and refrigerated.) Bake for 7 minutes.
5. Transfer rolls to heated plates and keep warm. Pour accumulated cooking juices into a skillet, bring to a boil, and reduce by one-half, about 3 minutes. Stir in cream, boil for 1 minute, and taste for seasoning. Pour sauce around fish.

QUAIL WITH CRACKED CORIANDER AND WILTED SPINACH SALAD

8 (4-ounce) quail, deboned, and cut in half
6 teaspoons coriander seeds
6 tablespoons olive oil, divided
Salt and pepper
2 tablespoons cognac
8 strips lean bacon, julienned
4 cups small spinach leaves, rinsed and thoroughly dried
1/2 cup Mustard Roquefort Vinaigrette (recipe follows)

1. Crack the coriander seeds coarsely, using a mortar and pestle or the base of a heavy skillet. Heat 1 tablespoon of the olive oil in a heavy skillet and sauté the coriander for 3 to 4 minutes.
2. Place quail halves in a shallow baking pan. Sprinkle with coriander, the remaining 5 tablespoons of olive oil, salt and pepper to taste, and cognac. Turn quail to coat well, and marinate at room temperature for 1 to 2 hours, covered with plastic wrap.
3. Just before serving, fry the bacon, and drain well on paper towels. Toss with spinach leaves and vinaigrette.
4. Preheat convection oven to 400 degrees. Roast quail for 6 minutes. Divide spinach salad among 8 plates. Cut each quail half into a leg and breast portion. Reassemble them on beds of spinach and serve at once.

MUSTARD ROQUEFORT VINAIGRETTE

1/4 teaspoon salt
2 tablespoons white or red wine vinegar, or fresh lemon juice
6 tablespoons virgin olive oil
Black pepper
1/2 teaspoon Dijon mustard
1 tablespoon crumbled Roquefort cheese
1 teaspoon finely chopped fresh thyme, tarragon, chives, basil, or parsley

1. In a small bowl, dissolve salt in vinegar. Beat in olive oil with a whisk. Add black pepper, Dijon mustard, Roquefort cheese, and fresh herb of your choice. Blend well. Taste for seasoning and adjust if necessary.

Makes 1/2 cup

HAZELNUT MERINGUE AND CHOCOLATE CREAM GATEAU

4 ounces whole hazelnuts, unpeeled
1/2 cup sugar, divided
4 large egg whites
Pinch salt
4 ounces semisweet or bittersweet chocolate, coarsely chopped
1 tablespoon cognac
2 tablespoons unsalted butter
3/4 cup heavy cream
1 cup chopped hazelnuts, lightly toasted, for decoration

1. Preheat convection oven to 325 degrees. Line a baking sheet with baking parchment, and mark off three 2 1/2 by 10-inch rectangles with a pencil. Stick the baking parchment to the baking sheet with dabs of butter at the corners. Have ready a pastry bag fitted with a plain round 1/4-inch tip.
2. Grind the hazelnuts to a powder, preferably in a nut mill, which makes fine flakes without releasing the nut oil. Combine the ground hazelnut powder with half of the sugar.
3. Beat egg whites until they start to hold their shape. Add salt and remaining sugar. Beat egg whites until very stiff. Lightly fold nut mixture into the meringue without deflating it.
4. Transfer the mixture into the pastry bag. Fill the 3 rectangles with meringue, piping the mixture in lines that touch each other. Bake for 20 minutes, or until crisp. Remove from the baking sheet and place onto a rack. (If meringue is difficult to remove, pour a little water under the paper to create steam on the hot baking sheet. Wait 2 minutes, then reverse paper onto the baking rack. The meringue layers will then peel off easily.)
5. Combine chocolate, cognac, and butter in a bowl or the top of a double boiler. Set over simmering water. When chocolate has melted, remove the mixture from the heat and let cool to barely lukewarm.
6. Whip the cream until it just starts to hold its shape. Add the chocolate mixture and whip together. (Do not overmix or you will make butter.)
7. Place 1 meringue layer flat side down on a serving plate, and cover with a layer of chocolate cream. Cover with a second layer of meringue and spread with cream. Top with the third layer of meringue, flat side up. Spread sides and top of cake

with chocolate cream. Make an S- shaped pattern on the top of the cake with a decorating comb or serrated knife. Scatter toasted chopped hazelnuts on sides of the cake and place on a serving platter. Refrigerate until serving time.

Makes 1 (10-inch) rectangular cake

Alice Waters has revolutionized the way America cooks. Her recipes, which turn up on America's tables, are often simple yet always comprised of the freshest fruits and vegetables grown in the California sun. She owns Chez Panisse in Berkeley, California, where many diners first experienced Goat Cheese Pizza, or Pasta with Sun Dried Tomatoes. Alice Waters is the author of *Chez Panisse Menu Cookbook* and co-author of *Chez Panisse Pasta, Pizza, and Calzone*.

On March 26, 1987, a special wine tasting was held in the Reading Terminal Market with dishes developed and prepared by Jill Horn, proprietor of Vorspeise, a specialty foods take out shop. The recipe for Chicken Fowlballs is Horn's creation.

The Reading Terminal Market is a United Nations of food and restaurants. Merchants sell their foodstuffs and wares in stalls, behind counters, or set up tables along the market's many aisles. For nearly 100 years, shoppers have flocked to the Reading Terminal Market, shopping bags in tow, and filled them with produce, cheese, fresh fish, meats, even a bottle of wine. The Amish farmers from Lancaster County set up shop Wednesday through Saturday, offering eggs, fowl, produce, and handmade pretzels.

The Reading Terminal Market is a bustling place where you can lunch on Mexican, Chinese, Italian, Japanese, and all American fare. During lunch, shoppers are serenaded by the local citizenry as musicians take their place at the piano or set up a bandstand for an afternoon of jazz.

MENU

FRESH FENNEL WITH OLIVE OIL

JUICY CALIFORNIA STRAWBERRIES

BLOOD ORANGE JUICE

ASSORTED CHEESES WITH CRACKERS

CHICKEN FOWLBALLS IN RED WINE SAUCE

1983 Iron Horse Sonoma County Brut Sparkling
1982 Montbray Winecellars Seyve Villard Maryland
1984 Eyrie Vineyards Pinot Noir, Reserve
1981 Chappellet Napa Cabernet Sauvignon

Serves 6

FRESH FENNEL WITH OLIVE OIL

3 bulbs fresh fennel
Olive oil for dipping
Kosher salt for dipping

1. Wash fennel bulbs under cold running water and dry thoroughly. Trim off the feathery ends, if you wish, and cut the fennel into 2-inch sticks. Serve on a platter with small bowls of olive oil and kosher salt for dipping.

JUICY CALIFORNIA STRAWBERRIES

2 pints ripe California strawberries
Small bowls of confectioners' sugar for dipping, optional
Strawberries soaked in several shots Grand Marnier, optional

1. Place strawberries in the refrigerator as soon as possible. When ready to serve, wash thoroughly and hull them.
2. Place in a large glass bowl with small bowls of confectioners' sugar for dipping.
3. Or add several shots of Grand Marnier or Cointreau to the bowl and allow to sit for several hours.
4. Or add 6 strawberries to flutes of champagne, one to a glass.

BLOOD ORANGE JUICE

Take several dozen blood oranges and squeeze for juice. Blood oranges have a very deep, red-orange color and would serve as a base for an interesting Mimosa if you add some champagne.

CHICKEN FOWLBALLS IN RED WINE SAUCE

For the Sauce:
1/2 cup butter
2 medium onions, diced
2 large cloves garlic, minced
6 tablespoons flour
1/2 teaspoon salt, or to taste
1/2 teaspoon pepper
4 cups hot chicken stock
1 cup red wine
1/2 cup parsley, minced
For the Fowlballs:
4 large boneless, skinless chicken breasts
1 cup bread crumbs
1/2 cup onion, finely diced
2 tablespoons parsley, minced
2 large eggs
1/2 teaspoon salt
1/4 teaspoon pepper, or to taste

1. Melt the butter over low-medium heat in a large, heavy bottom saucepan. Gently cook the onion and garlic for 3 to 5 minutes or until soft. Add the flour, salt, and pepper and stir until combined, cooking gently for 3 to 5 more minutes. Add the hot chicken stock, stirring or whisking to combine and prevent lumping of the flour mixture. Add the wine and keep sauce at a simmer.
2. As the sauce simmers, place chicken in work bowl of food processor fitted with the steel blade. Grind the chicken.
3. Place the ground chicken and remaining ingredients in a large bowl. Form small balls (the size of a walnut) and drop into the simmering sauce. The fowlballs will be sticky; you may wish to roll them in finely ground bread crumbs to help shape them.
4. Cook fowlballs gently, covered, for 20 minutes, adding salt and pepper as needed. Add chicken stock if sauce is too thick or has begun to evaporate. Simmer uncovered if sauce is too thin.

Makes 24 to 32 cocktail size fowlballs.

William Woys Weaver is a consultant who passes much of his time in the culinary past. As an historian, he spent many months researching his book *35 Receipts from The Larder Invaded*, an authenticated account of three centuries of Philadelphia food and drink. He owns his own firm, Food Research Nahrungsforschung, in Paoli, Pennsylvania.

On March 27, 1987, Weaver created this dinner at historic Valley Green Inn. The soup recipe is taken from *The Complete Cook*, by James Sanderson, published in 1843. The turkey recipe was developed by Philadelphia chef James W. Parkinson in 1852. The dessert recipe is from *The Larder Invaded*.

Valley Green Inn, established in 1683, may be the oldest restaurant in Philadelphia. Nestled along the Wissahickon Creek in Fairmount Park, Valley Green was a favorite dining spot of colonists, including Francis Daniel Pastorius, the first mayor of Germantown. It is believed that Benjamin Franklin stored his fine wines, port and Madeira in Valley Green's basement during the British occupation of Philadelphia.

Valley Green has low ceilings, polished hardwood floors, and tasteful antique furnishings. Patrons can dine outside on the porch in warmer months, just a stone's throw from the still standing livery where George Washington hitched his horse.

The menu changes with the season and may include baby coho or filet of salmon, homemade soups, game, veal, and pork.

SANDERSON'S PARSNIP SOUP

TURKEY WITH OYSTER SAUCE

NEW POTATOES BOILED IN THEIR SKINS

BUTTERED GREEN BEANS

BARNARD CAKE

Benjamin Franklin's Orange Shrub

Serves 8

SANDERSON'S PARSNIP SOUP

1 pound meaty veal bones
3 quarts water
2 teaspoons salt
1/2 teaspoon white pepper
1 small head celery, sliced (about 8 ounces)
1 onion, sliced (about 6 ounces)
4 tablespoons butter
6 large parsnips, pared and trimmed (about 2 pounds)
3/4 cup fine breadcrumbs (remove crust from bread)
Buttered croutons, optional
Sour cream, optional
Fresh chopped chives, optional
Salt and pepper to taste

1. Place bones, water, salt, and pepper in a large kettle and cook for 2 1/2 to 3 hours, or until broth is reduced to 2 quarts. Skim off the scum as it simmers, then strain out the bones.
2. Fry the celery and onion in butter in a large kettle. Add 2 quarts broth and parsnips. Cover and stew 1 1/2 hours. Strain and purée the vegetables in a processor. The purée must have a thick creamy consistency. Return this to the cooking broth.
3. Add the breadcrumbs and bring to a gentle boil for 2 to 3 minutes. Season with salt and pepper. Cool the soup and let stand overnight in the refrigerator to blend flavors. Reheat and serve the next day or serve cold. If served hot, it may be garnished with buttered croutons, if cold, with sour cream and fresh chopped chives.

TURKEY WITH OYSTER SAUCE

1 (8 to 10-pound) fresh or wild turkey
Strips of slab bacon to lard the turkey
4 tablespoons butter
2 tablespoons flour
1 pint fresh stewing oysters with liquor
1/2 teaspoon grated lemon or lime zest
3/4 teaspoon grated nutmeg
1/4 teaspoon mace
1 to 2 tablespoons lemon juice or champagne

1. Preheat the oven to 450 degrees. Wash and thoroughly dry turkey inside and outside. Place in a roasting pan. Either rub lard on outside of turkey or lay bacon strips on top of turkey. Reduce oven to 350 degrees and roast 25 minutes per pound, basting liberally from time to time with bacon or lard drippings.
2. In a large skillet, fry the flour and butter to make a blond roux. Add the oyster liquor, lemon or lime zest, nutmeg and mace. Stir and add the oysters. As the oysters are heating, add the lemon juice or champagne. Carve the turkey and when the oysters are hot, serve the sauce in a gravy boat.

BARNARD CAKE

1 cup butter
3 cups granulated sugar
4 eggs
1 cup buttermilk
Juice and grated zest of 1 lemon
4 1/2 cups pastry flour
1 1/4 teaspoons baking soda

1. Cream the butter and sugar until light and fluffy. Beat eggs to a froth and combine with the buttermilk. Beat the egg and butter mixtures together and add the lemon.
2. Sift together the flour and baking soda twice. Gradually sift and fold this into the batter. Grease 2 round 10-inch cake pans, preferably spring form, and fill no more than 2/3 full.
3. Bake in a preheated 350-degree oven for 45 to 50 minutes, or until the cake tests done. Cool on racks before removing from the pans.

Makes 1 (10-inch) cake

Anne Willan has studied and taught the fine art of cuisine in London, Paris, and Washington, D.C. She holds a Grand Diplôme du Cordon Bleu and conducted classes at London's Cordon Bleu Cookery School. She is a former associate editor of *Gourmet* and was food editor of the *Washington Star*. Willan is founder of L'École Cuisine LaVarenne in Paris and the author of several cookbooks including *French Regional Cooking*.

Willan created this dinner with Kathleen Mulhern, proprietor of The Garden, on March 22, 1985. The recipes are from *French Regional Cooking*.

The Garden, situated in an elegant late 19th century townhouse, offers splendid indoor dining in rooms whose walls offer an outstanding collection of English fruit and floral prints from the Victorian age. In warm weather, diners can sit in an outdoor pebble garden shaded by tall trees and handsome umbrellas. The Oyster Bar in The Garden, which occupies what was once a formal front parlor, offers patrons a wide selection of oysters, including Belon, Cotuit, Malpege, Long Island, and Wellfleet.

The menu is classic American and features prime grilled steaks, fish, seafood specialties, veal and crisp salads.

SELECTION OF OYSTERS

ESCALOPE OF VEAL WITH SHERRY VINEGAR AND BABY VEGETABLES

POTATOES AU GRATIN

NORMANDY APPLE TART

Champagne

Serves 6

SELECTION OF OYSTERS

36 oysters of your choice
Seaweed to serve as a bed
6 lemon wedges

1. Place dry oysters in the refrigerator until you are ready to open them.
2. Line 6 chilled plates with seaweed. Place open oysters on top of the seaweed in a circular manner. Garnish with lemon wedges.

ESCALOPE OF VEAL WITH SHERRY VINEGAR AND BABY VEGETABLES

For Vegetable Garnish:
1 pound baby carrots, peeled and trimmed, with a bit of top green
2 tablespoons butter, divided
3 teaspoons sugar, divided
Salt and pepper to taste
1 pound baby zucchini, trimmed and cut in large sticks, ends rounded
1 pound baby turnips, peeled and trimmed, with a bit of top green and cut into wedges
1 pound baby onions, peeled
1 small bunch chives
For the Veal:
6 veal escalopes, cut in 2 to 3 pieces
2 to 3 tablespoons flour seasoned with salt and pepper
2 tablespoons butter (for frying)
3 tablespoons veal stock
3 tablespoons sherry vinegar
1 cup cold butter, cut in pieces
1 tablespoon chopped fresh chervil or basil

1. Place the carrots in cold water to cover with 1/2 tablespoon butter, 1 teaspoon sugar, salt, and pepper. Boil, uncovered, until carrots are tender and water has evaporated, leaving a shiny glaze.
2. Place zucchini in a large pan of boiling water and blanch 2 minutes. Drain, refresh under cold water, and drain thoroughly.
3. Cook turnips and onions separately, as for carrots. Pick out 12 strips of chive and blanch in boiling water 1 minute, then drain. Chives and vegetables can be prepared up to 4 hours ahead and refrigerated. Shortly before serving, reheat all vegetables separately, using remaining 1/2 tablespoon of butter to lightly fry zucchini without browning.
4. To finish: Coat veal with seasoned flour, patting off excess. In a large frying pan melt half of the butter and fry half the escalopes over brisk heat until brown, 1 to 2 minutes on each side. Remove and keep warm. Fry remaining escalopes in remaining butter and keep warm.
5. For sauce: Discard all fat from frying pan, leaving 3 tablespoons veal stock. Add vinegar and boil, stirring to dissolve pan juices. Boil until reduced by half. Take pan from heat and whisk in cold butter, working alternately on and off the heat so butter softens

and emulsifies without melting to oil. Strain sauce and taste for seasoning.

6. Arrange veal on individual plates with vegetables around the edge. Sprinkle zucchini with basil or chervil. Spoon sauce over veal and lay 2 strips of chive on top. Serve at once.

NORMANDY APPLE TART

For the Pastry:
1 1/2 cups flour
6 tablespoons butter
1 egg yolk
1/2 teaspoon salt
4 to 5 tablespoons cold water
For the Apples:
3 to 4 Golden Delicious apples
Sugar (for sprinkling)
1/2 cup apricot glaze
For the Frangipane:
6 tablespoons butter
1/2 cup sugar
1 egg
1 egg yolk
1 tablespoon calvados or applejack
2/3 cup blanched whole almonds, ground
2 tablespoons flour

1. Sift the flour onto a work surface and make a large well in the center. Put the butter, egg yolk, salt, and 4 tablespoons of water in the well, and work together with the fingertips until partly mixed. Gradually draw in the flour, working the dough lightly between the fingers so it forms large crumbs. If some dry crumbs remain that don't stick together to form large ones, sprinkle up to 1 tablespoon additional water over them.
2. Press the dough together into a ball. It should be soft but not sticky. Now, on a floured surface, push a portion of the dough away from you with the heel of the hand in a long sliding motion. Work all of the pastry in this way and then gather it together again with a dough scraper.
3. Repeat this process, if necessary, continuing until the dough is completely mixed, smooth and pliable. Press the dough into a ball, wrap and chill for at least 15 minutes. It can be stored, wrapped and refrigerated, for up to 3 days, or it can be frozen.
4. Butter a 10-inch tart pan. Roll the dough on a floured surface to a sheet 3/16-inch thick, and line the tart pan with the dough. Chill until firm, at least 15 minutes. The tart shell can be shaped up to 3 days ahead.
5. For the frangipane: Cream the butter, gradually beat in the sugar and continue beating until the mixture is light and soft. Beat in the egg and then the yolk. Add the calvados or applejack and

then stir in the ground almonds and the flour. The frangipane can be made up to 4 hours ahead and kept, covered, in the refrigerator.

6. Heat the oven to 400 degrees. Spread the frangipane in the bottom of the chilled pastry shell. Peel the apples, halve them and scoop out the cores. Cut each half crosswise into very thin slices and arrange them on the frangipane like the spokes of a wheel. Press them down gently until they touch the base of the tart.
7. Bake the tart in the bottom third of the hot oven until the pastry begins to brown, 10 to 15 minutes. Lower the oven heat to 350 degrees and cook until the apples are tender and the frangipane is set, 15 to 20 minutes.
8. Ten minutes before the end of cooking, sprinkle the tart with sugar and continue cooking until the sugar melts and caramelizes slightly. Transfer to a rack. When the tart is cool, melt the apricot glaze and brush the top of the tart with it. Serve at room temperature.

It has been said of Paula Wolfert that "she understands cooking like Rubinstein understands Chopin." Although she calls New York City home, Wolfert spent several years living and carefully studying the art of cuisine in Morocco and Paris. She is a teacher, perfectionist cook, and author of *Couscous and Other Good Food from Morocco*, *The Cooking of Southwest France* and *Paula Wolfert's World of Food.*

Wolfert and Chef Gary Bachman created the following dinner at Odéon on March 18, 1988. The recipes are from *The Cooking of Southwest France.*

Stepping into Odéon, located in the heart of Philadelphia's central business district, is to arrive in a sophisticated French bistro. A two-tiered restaurant, Odéon, named for the famous Métro stop in Paris, is visually dominated by a grand sweeping staircase and large wall mirrors that enhance its continental atmosphere.

Odéon's cuisine is strongly flavored and imaginative. It derives much of its inspiration from the regional cooking of Southwest France. The restaurant specializes in new and unusual French wines, many of which are available by the glass from the cruvinet.

ANCHOVY-OLIVE DIP

(Tapenade de Toulouse)

With Toasted French Bread

ALAIN DUTOURNIER'S DUCK BREASTS
WITH CAPERS AND MARROW

(Magret de Canard aux Capres et a la Moelle)

STEAMED NEW POTATOES

FRESH FRUIT SORBET

Cahors

Serves 4

ANCHOVY-OLIVE DIP *(Tapenade de Toulouse)*

1 (2-ounce) can anchovy fillets packed in oil, drained, or 2 salt-packed anchovies (see Note)
18 pitted oil-cured or salted black olives, soaked overnight in olive oil with slivers of garlic
1 tablespoon Dijon mustard
1 egg yolk
1/2 cup fruity olive oil
1 tablespoon fresh strained lemon juice
Cayenne pepper

1. Place anchovies in small bowl with cold water to cover; let soak 20 minutes; drain.
2. Combine anchovies, olives, and mustard in work bowl of food processor fitted with metal blade or in electric blender; using on-off motion, process until coarsely chopped, scraping down sides of bowl as necessary.
3. Add egg yolk; blend thoroughly until smooth. With machine on, add oil in a slow, steady stream. Add lemon juice; season to taste with cayenne. Spoon into 1-cup crock. Tapenade de Toulouse can be refrigerated, covered, up to 3 days.

Serve with toasted French bread.

Makes about 3/4 cup.

NOTE: If using salted anchovies, soak them in cold water 2 hours. With a small knife, remove fillets, rinse thoroughly and pat dry. Use all 8 fillets.

ALAIN DUTOURNIER'S DUCK BREASTS WITH CAPERS AND MARROW
(Magret de Canard aux Capres et a la Moelle)

Begin 1 to 2 days in advance
2 whole duck breasts, halved, boned, excess fat removed, skin intact
For the Spice Paste:
1 tablespoon juniper berries
1/2 tablespoon black peppercorns
1 (1-inch) stick cinnamon
1/2 teaspoon freshly grated nutmeg
1 clove
1 1/2 tablespoon Izarra or green Chartreuse liqueur
1 tablespoon Dijon mustard
3/4 teaspoon coarse (kosher) salt
For the Marrowbones:
This amount should yield 12 inches of marrow (about 4 bones)
1/4 cup red wine vinegar
1/2 cup red dry white wine
2 1/2 cups demi-glacé or duck demi-glacé
3 tablespoons unsalted butter
1/3 cup nonpareil capers, drained
2 tablespoons unsalted butter
1/3 cup nonpareil capers, drained
2 tablespoons snipped fresh chives

1. Begin 1 to 2 days in advance marinating the duck, soaking marrow and making the sauce base. Pat duck breasts dry with paper towels. Make the spice paste: In a dry skillet over low heat toast the juniper berries until shiny, about 2 minutes (this brings out their flavor).
2. Transfer to spice mill or mortar. Add peppercorns, cinnamon, nutmeg, and clove; grind to a fine powder. Sift if necessary. You should have about 1 1/2 tablespoons spice mixture. Set aside 4 teaspoons for the sauce. Transfer remaining powder to a wide, noncorrodible bowl. Add liqueur, mustard, and salt. Blend to a paste.
3. Rub duck breasts with the spice paste. Stack seasoned duck breasts in the same bowl and cover with plastic wrap. Refrigerate 24 hours or more, turning the duck breasts daily.
4. Rinse marrowbones under cold running water; place in a bowl and cover with warm water. Let stand 3 to 5 minutes. Drain well. Using a skewer, loosen the marrow from the bones, then

push marrow out in whole pieces into small bowl of cold salted water. (This helps marrow to rid itself of any blood. Marrow will keep fresh for 2 to 3 days.)

5. Make the sauce: Combine reserved 4 teaspoons spice powder with vinegar and wine in small, noncorrodible saucepan; bring to a boil over medium-high heat. Let boil until reduced by half. Add demi-glacé and bring to a boil. Boil slowly with pan half off the heat, skimming often, until sauce is reduced to 1 1/4 cups, about 30 minutes. Sauce can be prepared ahead up to this point. Cool, cover and refrigerate.

6. 30 minutes before serving: preheat the oven to 350 degrees. Remove duck from refrigerator and dry with paper towels. Score skin at 3/4-inch intervals without piercing flesh.

7. 15 minutes before serving: transfer duck, skin side down, to heavy skillet. Place over high heat and sauté until skin is crisp and brown, about 2 to 3 minutes. Transfer breasts to a baking sheet and place in the oven to finish cooking - about 6 to 7 minutes, or until meat is pink and just firm when pressed with fingertip. Set aside.

8. Meanwhile, pour off fat from skillet and stir over medium-high heat, scraping up any browned bits that cling to bottom and sides of pan. Strain sauce through fine sieve. Return to skillet and keep below a simmer to avoid evaporation.

9. Cut marrow into 3/4-inch chunks. In small saucepan, bring 1 1/2 cups salted water to a boil. Reduce heat to low, add marrow and gently poach until pale pink-gray in color, about 2 minutes. Immediately transfer marrow to flat dish to drain. Do not leave in water or marrow will melt.

10. Remove duck breasts from the oven and place on a carving board. Let rest 1 to 2 minutes. Meanwhile, swirl butter into sauce, 1 tablespoon at a time. Stir in the capers. Taste and adjust seasoning. Cut duck into thin slices diagonally. Arrange on individual hot serving plates. Spoon sauce over slices. Top with marrow, dividing pieces evenly among servings. Sprinkle with chives.

Eileen Yin-Fei Lo & Susanna Foo

Eileen Yin-Fei Lo is versed in every aspect of Chinese cuisine. She is a prominent teacher and world traveler whose commentary on food, wine, and travel appears in the *New York Times* and *Travel & Leisure*. Born in Canton, China where she took her first cooking classes, she also studied in Hong Kong. She is currently an instructor at the China Institute of America in New York City.

Eileen Yin-Fei Lo lives in Montclair, New Jersey, with her husband, *Gourmet* columnist Fred Feretti and her family.

Her cookbooks include *Dim Sum* and the award-winning *Chinese Banquet Cookbook* which features authentic feasts from China's regions. Her newest collection is the *New Cantonese Cookbook*, on which this dinner, served on March 18, 1988 at Susanna Foo, is based.

Chef Susanna Foo, recently named one of America's top ten women chefs by *USA Today*, creates Chinese dishes with a French flair. This type of cuisine, known as *Chinoise Francais*, has become popular in the United States. Foo is responsible for making it famous in Philadelphia. The restaurant which bears her name is located in the heart of center city. The ambience is understated elegance; white linen, black furniture, deep mauve banquettes, and an abundance of fresh flowers.

Among Foo's specialties are a selection of dim sum, including Steamed Seafood Dumplings in a delicate coriander sauce or fried and stuffed with veal. The Hot and Sour Soup is rich and lightly spiced. Main courses include Giant Prawns; Sliced Filet of Beef; and a Whole Fresh Bass, steamed or crisply fried.

Vintages from California, Italy and France are choices from the wine list and, of course, Chinese beer.

MENU

WON TUN WITH VEAL

(Won Tun Jai Yuk)

DUCK AND MELON SALAD

(Mut Gua Op Sah Lud)

FILLET OF BEEF ROASTED IN SATAY SAUCE

(Gah Lei Ngau Lau Yuk)

RICE

(Fon)

FRESH FRUIT IN SEASON

Oolong Tea
Chinese Rice Wine
Serves 6

DUCK AND MELON SALAD
(Mut Gua Op Sah Lud)

3/4 cup roasted duck meat, julienned
1 1/2 tablespoons crushed dry-roasted peanuts
3/4 cup julienned cantalope
1/4 cup julienned celery
1/3 cup julienned carrot
1/4 cup julienned scallions, white portions only
1/2 teaspoon salt
1 teaspoon sugar
3/4 teaspoon light soy sauce
1 tablespoon sesame oil
1 1/4 teaspoons white vinegar
1/2 teaspoon Shao-Hsing wine or sherry
Pinch of white pepper
Oranges (for a garnish)

1. Place all the ingredients except the oranges in a large mixing bowl. Mix together thoroughly. Cover and refrigerate for 4 hours. Serve cool, in a dish garnished with half-moon slices of fresh oranges arranged in scallops around edge of serving dish.

WON TUN WITH VEAL
(Won Tun Ngau Jai Yuk)

For the Won Tun Skins:
3 cups bleached, high-gluten flour
1 1/4 teaspoons baking soda
1 teaspoon salt (optional)
4 extra-large eggs
1/4 cup water
2/3 cup of cornstarch, for dusting
For the Filling:
3/4 pound ground veal
1 1/2 cups Chinese chives, or regular chives, washed, dried, with 1/8 inch trimmed off the white end, and cut into 1/4-inch dice
1/4 pound shrimp, shelled, deveined, washed in salt water, dried, and cut into 1/4-inch dice
1/4 cup bamboo shoots, cut into 1/4-inch dice
1 teaspoon grated ginger mixed with 1 1/2 teaspoons Shao-Hsing wine or sherry
1 1/2 teaspoons minced garlic
3/4 teaspoon salt
1 1/4 teaspoons sugar
1 1/2 teaspoons dark soy sauce
2 teaspoons sesame oil
1 tablespoon peanut oil
1 tablespoon oyster sauce
2 1/2 tablespoons cornstarch
Pinch of white pepper
1 medium egg

1. To make the won tun skins, place the flour on a work surface and mix with the baking soda and salt. Make a well in the center and add the eggs, unbeaten. Work the dough with your fingers until the eggs are absorbed. Slowly drizzle the water into the dough, mixing with your hands as you do, until it is thoroughly blended. Use a dough scraper to collect the excess pieces. Then begin to knead the dough.
2. Knead for about 10 minutes, or until dough becomes elastic, then set aside, covered with a damp cloth, for 3 hours.
3. When the dough is ready, dust the work surface with cornstarch. Divide the dough into 2 equal pieces. Roll each piece with a rolling pin until you have a sheet 1/4-inch thick. Pick up sheet, dust the surface again, and roll again, continually, until the dough's thickness is reduced to 1/8 inch, or less.

4. Roll up the dough around a length of broom handle or a dowel. Dust the work surface again. Roll the dough off the broom handle, then roll with the rolling pin again, as thin as possible, then again roll up around broom handle to lift it from the work surface. You must use the broom handle, or dowel, because otherwise the dough will tear.
5. Dust the work surface again, unroll the sheet onto it, and with rolling pin, roll out a sheet about 18 by 21 inches. Repeat with the second piece of dough.
6. Cut the won tun. Before cutting, make certain the surface is dusted again. Using the edge of the dough scraper, cut squares 3 inches by 3 inches. Reserve the skins for use.

NOTE: When freshly made, the skins cannot be used because they are brittle. Store overnight, refrigerated and wrapped in plastic to renew elasticity. Be certain that there is a dusting of cornstarch between all skins. The skins can be frozen for 4 to 6 weeks. Defrost and allow to come to room temperature before using.

Makes 100 won tun skins. Use 30 for this recipe.

7. To make the filling, combine all ingredients in a large mixing bowl and stir clockwise.
8. Skins should be kept in plastic wrap at room temperature. Twenty minutes before preparation, peel off the plastic wrap and cover the skins with a wet towel.
9. Keeping a bowl of water at hand so that the 4 edges of the won tun can be wetted, place about 1 tablespoon of the mixture on the nonfloured side of the skin. Then the skin should be folded and squeezed along the wet edges so it seals like an envelope.
10. Once it is folded and sealed, the 2 corners of the folded sides are wetted and then drawn together and squeezed with the fingers to create a bowlike dumpling. As each won tun is made, place it on a floured cookie sheet so that it will not stick.
11. Cook the won tun in 3 quarts of water to which have been added 2 tablespoons of salt and 1 tablespoon of peanut oil. The water should be boiling before the won tun are placed in it. The usual cooking time is 5 to 7 minutes, or until the won tun become translucent and the filling can be seen through the skin. Use a wooden spoon to stir 3 or 4 times during cooking to avoid sticking. Cook in 2 batches.
12. Remove pot of won tun from heat and run cold water into it. Drain. Run more cold water through the won tun. Drain again. Place them on waxed paper and allow them to dry.

Makes 30 won tun

NOTE: Won tun can be pan-fried, deep-fat-fried, steamed, or put into soup. Eileen Yin-Fei Lo likes to serve them as a first course with a spicy sauce.

To Make the Sauce, Mix Together:
1 1/2 teaspoons white vinegar
1 teaspoon sugar
Pinch of white pepper
4 teaspoons Shao-Hsing wine or sherry
4 teaspoons dark soy sauce
1 tablespoon sesame oil
1 tablespoon chili oil
1/2 teaspoon chopped fresh coriander
1/2 teaspoon chopped white portions of scallions
1 teaspoon minced garlic

Simply pour this over the boiled won tun and serve.

Leftover won tun skins can be frozen for future use. Double-wrap them in plastic wrap and aluminum foil. Won tun can be frozen as well. Be certain they are thoroughly dry, then double-wrap in plastic and aluminum foil. Completely defrost before using.

FILLET OF BEEF ROASTED IN SATAY SAUCE
(Gah Lei Ngau Lau Yuk)

1 (2-pound) center-cut beef tenderloin, 9 to 10 inches long
1/2 cup dark soy sauce
2 1/2 tablespoons curry powder, preferably Madras
Pinch white pepper
1/3 cup honey
2 tablespoons peanut oil

1. With the back of a knife, make 6 equally spaced marks crosswise on the beef fillet to divide it into equal portions. With a sharp knife or Chinese cleaver, cut 2/3 of the way through the meat at the markings.
2. In a small bowl, mix together the soy sauce, curry powder, white pepper, and honey.
3. Place the beef in a shallow roasting pan and pour the marinade over it. With your hands, rub the marinade into the meat on the outside and in the cuts. Cover with plastic wrap and refrigerate overnight. About 1 hour before cooking, remove the meat from the refrigerator and let stand, basting frequently with the marinade as the meat returns to room temperature.
4. Preheat the oven to 500 degrees. Rub the beef with the peanut oil and roast, basting with the marinade in the pan every 5 minutes for 15, 20, or 25 minutes depending on your preference for rare, medium, or well-done meat. Add 2 tablespoons of water to the pan if the sauce begins to dry out. Cut the meat into the slices indicated by the cuts and pour a little sauce on each. Serve the remaining sauce in a boat on the side.

Permissions

The Food of Portugal, William Morrow and Company. Copyright 1985 by Jean Anderson. Reprinted by permission of the author.

Joe's Book of Mushroom Cookery, MacMillan Publishing. Copyright 1988 by Jack Czarnecki. Reprinted by permission of the author.

Italian Fast and Fresh, Harper & Row. Copyright 1984 by Julie Dannenbaum. Reprinted by permission of the author.

Recipes From the Badia, Copyright Lorenza de' Medici. Reprinted by permission of the author.

Lord Krishna's Cuisine: The Art of Indian Vegetarian Cooking, Bala Books. Copyright 1987 by Yamuna Devi. Reprinted by permission of the author.

New Southern Cooking, Alfred A. Knopf. Copyright 1986 by Nathalie Dupree. Reprinted by permission of the author.

Pleasures of the Table, Gordon Press. Copyright 1989 by Florence Fabricant. Reprinted by permission of the author.

The Encyclopedia of Cajun & Creole Cuisine, the Encyclopedia Cookbook Committee, Donaldsonville, Louisiana. Copyright John D. Folse and the Committee, 1983. Reprinted by permission of the author.

Seafood Cookery Classic to Contemporary, Times Books. Copyright 1986, Pierre Franey and Bryan Miller. Reprinted by permission of the author.

International Slim Gourmet, copyright Barbara Gibbons. Reprinted by permission of the author.

Greene on Greens, Workman Publishing. Copyright 1984 by Bert Greene. Reprinted by permission of the author.

Kitchen Bouquets, Contemporary Books, Inc. Copyright 1979 by Bert Greene. Reprinted by permission of the author.

Vibration Cooking, copyright by Vertamae Grosvenor.

Viennese Cuisine, The New Approach, Doubleday. Copyright 1987 by Peter Grunauer. Reprinted by permission of the author.

Hot Stuff: A Cookbook in Praise of the Piquant, Atheneum Publishers, Inc. Copyright 1985 by Jessica B. Harris. Reprinted by permission of the author.

Maida Heatter's Book of Great Desserts, Alfred A. Knopf. Copyright 1974 by Maida Heatter. Reprinted by permission of the author.

East Meets West Cuisine, Simon & Schuster. Copyright 1987 by Ken Hom. Reprinted by permission of the author.

Cucina Fresca, Harper & Row. Copyright 1985 by Evan Kleiman and Viana La Place. Reprinted by permission of the authors.

Pasta Fresca, William Morrow and Company. Copyright 1988 by Evan Kleiman and Viana La Place. Reprinted by permission of the authors.

Reading Between the Recipes, Yankee Books. Copyright 1987 by Leslie Land. Reprinted by permission of the author.

The Greens Cookbook, Bantam Books. Copyright 1987 by Edward Espe Brown and Deborah Madison. Reprinted by permission of the author.

Ismail Merchant's Indian Cuisine, St. Martins Press. Copyright 1986 by Ismail Merchant. Reprinted by permission of the author.

The Food of Southern Italy, William Morrow and Company. Copyright 1987 by Carlo Middione. Reprinted by permission of the author.

The Art of Cooking, Alfred A. Knopf. Copyright 1988 by Jacques Pepin. Reprinted by permission of the author.

The New Italian Cooking, Little Brown and Company. Copyright 1980 by Margaret and G. Franco Romagnoli. Reprinted by permission of the authors.

The Easy Gourmet, copyright by Irene Rothschild. Reprinted by permission of the author.

Ethnic Cuisine: The Flavor Principle Cookbook, The Stephen Greene Press. Copyright 1983 by Elisabeth Rozin. Reprinted by permission of the author.

Desserts, Harper & Row. Copyright 1986 by Nancy Silverton. Reprinted by permission of the author.

The Philadelphia Neighborhood Cookbook, Camino Books. Copyright 1987 by Irina Smith and Ann Hazan. Reprinted by permission of the authors.

Convection Cuisine, Hearst Books. Copyright 1988 by René Verdon and Jacqueline Mallorca. Reprinted by permission of the authors.

The Larder Invaded, The Library Company of Philadelphia. Copyright 1987. Reprinted by permission of the author.

French Regional Cooking, copyright by Anne Willan. Reprinted by permission of the author.

The Cooking of Southwest-France, The Dial Press. Copyright 1983 by Paula Wolfert. Reprinted by permission of the author.

New Cantonese Cooking, Viking. Copyright 1988 by Eileen Yin-Fei Lo. Reprinted by permission of the author.

Index